Secrets of
First Love
Unique and Lasting Intimate Relationship For Christian Couples

Sam Sebastian Khor

Copyright ©2013 by Sam Sebastian Khor

All rights reserved. No part of this publication may be produced, stored in a retrieval system, or transmitted in any form or by any means—for example, electronic, photocopy, and recording— without prior written permission of the author. The only exception is brief quotations in printed reviews.

Printed by CreateSpace, an Amazon.com Company.

Library of Congress Cataloguing-in-Publication Data

Author: Sam Sebastian Khor
Editing and e-book services: ChristianEditingServices.com

ISBN-13: 978-1499144611
ISBN-10: 149914461X

Unless otherwise indicated, Scripture quotations are taken from the King James Version 2000 of the Bible, editor Robert A. Couric, Doctor of Theology and Retired Professor of Bible at Mid-Continent University in Mayfield, Kentucky.

Scripture quotations identified as NKJV are taken from the New King James Version. Copyright ©1979, 1980, 1982 by Thomas Nelson, Inc. Used by permission. All rights reserved.

Scripture quotations identified as ISV are taken from the Holy Bible: International Standard Version® Release 2.0. Copyright © 1996–2010 by the ISV Foundation. Used by permission of Davidson Press, LLC. ALL RIGHTS RESERVED INTERNATIONALLY.

Scripture quotations identified as NIV are taken from the HOLY BIBLE, NEW INTERNATIONAL VERSION®. NIV®. Copyright © 1973, 1978, 1984 by International Bible Society. Used by permission of Zondervan. All rights reserved.

Scripture quotations identified as NASB are taken from the New American Standard Bible®, Copyright © 1960, 1962, 1963, 1968, 1971, 1972, 1973, 1975, 1977, 1995 by The Lockman Foundation. Used by permission.

Scripture quotations identified as NRSV are taken from the New Revised Standard Version of the Bible, copyright 1989, Division of Christian Education of the National Council of the Churches of Christ in the United States of America. Used by permission. All rights reserved.

TABLE OF CONTENTS

ACKNOWLEDGMENTS IX

PREFACE XI

A NOTE ON HOW THE BOOK IS ORGANIZED XV

A NOTE ON BIBLE VERSIONS XVI

CHAPTER 1: WHAT IS THE PROBLEM? 1

    SUMMARY 11

CHAPTER 2: LOVE: OBEDIENCE AND SURVIVAL IN GENESIS 1 13

    NAME OF GOD: GOD 15

    CREATION OF HUMANS 17

    SURVIVAL AND MALE AND FEMALE ROLES 18

    THE TEN COMMANDMENTS AND MARRIAGE 30

    SUMMARY 34

CHAPTER 3: LOVE: SACRIFICE AND SUBMISSION IN GENESIS 2 37

    THE ORDER OF CREATION 40

    NAME OF GOD: LORD GOD 44

    THE CREATION REVISITED 45

    THE PLOT 51

    THE DOWNFALL 54

    THE GARDEN OF LOVE 56

    THE GREAT MYSTERY 59

    BOND BUILDING 80

        Head and Body 81

        Sacrificial Love 88

Submissive Love *91*

The Love Mission 102

Summary 108

CHAPTER 4: SPIRITUAL MATURITY AND MULTIPLICATION (CIRCUMCISION) 111

Spiritual Survival and Multiplication 112

Origin of Spiritual Multiplication 121

Physical Circumcision 131

   Male Circumcision *131*

   Neonatal Circumcision *140*

   Female Circumcision *143*

Summary 144

CHAPTER 5: PHYSICAL INTIMACY: THE ANATOMY 147

Male Reproductive System 149

Female Reproductive System 155

CHAPTER 6: PHYSICAL INTIMACY: ONENESS 163

Love Versus Lust 165

Sexual Temptations 169

Phases of the Sexual Response Cycle 176

   Desire *177*

   Arousal *177*

   Plateau *179*

   Orgasm and Ejaculation *181*

   Resolution *189*

Effects of Circumcision 189

Circumcision of the Heart and Emotions 193

Summary 201

CHAPTER 7: PHYSICAL INTIMACY: A BIBLICAL PICTURE 203

- STUDY APPROACH 205
- PROLOGUE 211
  - *A poem and a play* 212
  - *Prelude* 213
  - *A Play within a Play* 214
  - *Mosaic Laws* 215
  - *Vineyard* 215
  - *Mother* 216
  - *Circumcision* 216
- THE SONG 217
- SUMMARY 269

CHAPTER 8: CONCLUSION 271

INDEX 279

REFERENCE 286

Acknowledgments

This book has evolved over many years. During these years, I have been indebted to many, only a few of whom I can acknowledge in this space. I gratefully acknowledge and appreciate Jarl Waggoner for his diligent, professional, and skillful editorial work. The book would not have been completed in such a timely manner without his uncompromising critiques and thoroughness in execution. Restructuring arguments, turning some difficult explanations into plain English, and swift response are his strengths. My gratitude goes to Pastor Neilson for his vital theological knowledge, which has shaped some of the arguments and interpretations. Furthermore, he also contributed toward the preliminary editing work. During the long journey since 2000, the knowledge accumulated from many people is too vast to properly list here. It is remarkable how God has guided me through these years. Credit also should go to those who reviewed the manuscript.

PREFACE

Early in my Christian life, I often struggled to make sense of the apparent disparity in the messages of the Scriptures, especially in regard to men and women. For example, on the one hand, it seems clear in the Bible that God created men and women as equals. On the other hand, the Bible also teaches very clearly that the wife is to submit to her husband. I could not make sense of these differences or reconcile what seemed to be two contradictory views. While many Christians appeared to lean heavily to one side or the other, others sought a middle ground, which seemed the logical thing to do. However, I could not convince myself there was a "middle ground" in the Bible. So the struggle went on for many years. Are men and women created as equals or not? Should wives be submissive? What does this submission really mean? What does it mean for the husband to be the *head* of the wife? The more I struggled with these issues, the more questions arose. I found myself stuck in these apparent "contradictions" without much hope of finding a satisfactory solution.

All these years there was no doubt in my mind that God exists and that the Bible is inspired by the Holy

Spirit. Yet I found myself challenged by my own faith and the questions raised by certain biblical passages. The answers seemed elusive.

In the year 2000, however, I began to see the Scriptures differently. I observed that often we actually do not practice what is taught in the Scriptures. In fact, we even choose to bear our own "little" cross rather than the yoke Jesus wants us to carry.

> *Take my [Jesus'] yoke upon you, and learn of me; for I am meek and lowly in heart: and you shall find rest unto your souls. For my yoke is easy, and my burden is light.*
> *Matthew 11:29–30*

It was a journey of great challenges and perseverance as I tried to learn from Jesus.

In 2007 I was especially struck by the story of Moses preparing the Israelites for their circumcision before they crossed into the Promised Land. I had read this story many times before, but for the first time the Lord opened my eyes to truly understand it.

> *And the LORD your God will circumcise your heart, and the heart of your descendants, to love the LORD your God with all your heart, and with all your soul, that you may live.*
> *Deuteronomy 30:6*

I marveled at what Moses said concerning circumcision of the heart (Deuteronomy 30:6) compared to what actually was executed—circumcision of the penis (Joshua 5). Somehow this circumcision seemed to link to love. I spent another year and a half researching this and discovered that circumcision is indeed connected to love. I decided I would devote the rest of my life to Jesus and be circumcised according to the circumcision performed on Abraham and the ancient Jews.

That marked a turning point in my life. The bits and pieces of the jigsaw puzzles I had gathered over the years suddenly seemed to fit together. All the questions I had asked were resolved. I was grateful for being given the gift of understanding the Bible like never before.

One Sunday in June 2011, as I continued my daily Bible study in the book of Song of Songs, God opened my eyes. Suddenly the lyrics in the Song became very plain, and the secrets that had been hidden from me were now quite vivid. It took me quite a while to digest and put together my thoughts about this book and complete my study of it.

My new understanding of Song of Songs seemed to tie in with what the apostle Paul calls a great mystery in Ephesians 5:32. That mystery concerns Christ and the church. The love relationship between Christ and his church is to be reflected in the lives of husbands and wives, as Paul made clear in the chapter.

This book is an attempt to bring together these various threads of biblical teaching on love and marriage in order to address the great challenges marriages face today. The first chapter examines the evolution of traditional marriage ideology and its practices, expectations, and goals in light of the breakdown of marriage today. We then study how God revealed his great love plan for humanity, beginning with the first love he established with the creation of Adam and Eve. Along the way, we will discover the secrets of that first love in obedience to God, sacrifice and submission in marriage, and spiritual maturity and multiplication. God's love plan also includes physical intimacy. The book of Song of Songs marks the ultimate highlight of this aspect of marriage.

This is not a book on marriage counseling or a guide to marital reconciliation. It is not a sex guide either, although there are many sexual references and descriptions in the Scriptures to guide husbands and wives in their sexual expressions. Rather, it is a study of the "secrets" of love God intended for couples to know and practice in order to experience God's best for them.

For those who are contemplating matrimony, as well as those who want to reenergize their marriages, this book provides essential biblical information for establishing a meaningful and happy marriage that is blessed by God. It will equip couples with knowledge of their proper roles and attitudes and of sexual techniques they will find useful. It alerts couples to the influences that can break down nuptial happiness and reveals the secrets of staying happily married as God intended. This book presents a fresh look at the purpose of marriage and hopefully will empower readers to lead purpose-filled, meaningful lives with God at the center.

A Note on How the Book Is Organized

The main contents of the book are written in normal font size and style. Interspersed throughout are biblical quotations. These are written in italics with the book name, chapter, and verse number(s) following. For example:

> *For God so loved the world, that he gave his only begotten Son, that whosoever believes in him should not perish, but have everlasting life.*
> John 3:16

Sometimes, for clarity, it is necessary to include in biblical quotations additional words that are not in the original text. These are included in square brackets, as follows:

> *If I [Jesus] have told you earthly things, and you believe not, how shall you believe, if I tell you of heavenly things?*
> John 3:12

The book is organized into eight chapters. The chapters should be read in proper sequence, as each chapter builds on information presented in previous chapters.

A Note on Bible Versions

There are many Bible versions, or translations, available today. Each one has its own merits and weaknesses, and none can claim to be a *perfect* translation. It is important, however, to have a very accurate and reliable translation, and, undeniably, the King James Version is that. For simplicity and ease of reading, the King James Version 2000 (KJ2000) is quoted extensively in this book. Where other versions are quoted, an abbreviation of the version is affixed. These include the New King James Version (NKJV), the International Standard Version (ISV), the New International Version (NIV), and the New American Standard Bible (NASB). I also refer to the original texts (Hebrew and Greek) when the semantics are clearly lost in translation or further explanation is needed. The phonetic forms of Greek and Hebrew words are given in parentheses.

Chapter 1

What Is the Problem?

What therefore God has joined together, let not man put asunder.
Matthew 19:6

It's nearly time for dessert, and the evening has flown by. You can't remember a second date that's gone so smoothly and so quickly. The wines, the entrées, and the settings in the restaurant were magnificent. You're sure you could dine out every night with this person without so much as a minor culinary squabble. You wish this day could continue forever. You dream of a few years down the trek and imagine this loved one is still with you. You love and cherish one another. You are still dining out together and still holding hands, and a few lovely children are playing on the lawn. If only you could gaze into the future through a crystal ball to determine if this person is indeed the "one"! But there is no crystal ball, so you just make a bold decision and take the plunge. There is no one better. He or she has to be the one!

A few years later, you find how off the mark you were, as you recount in your mind the all-too-familiar conversation you just had with your other half.

"Are you coming to bed?"

"Just a little later," came the familiar reply.

Outwardly, the two sentences sound so mundane and inconsequential, but their meanings have become transparent.

"I need you."

"No, I don't need you."

How things have changed. You never hold hands anymore. "Home" is no more a longed-for attraction.

You seem to know each other very well—the bad habits, the tempers, the next moves, the routines, the laziness, the sloppiness, and so on—and yet you are like strangers sharing the same bed. Evenings are now boring and lonely. Your voices are no longer music to each other's ears, and you cannot even earn enough to pay the bills. How you wish the clock could be turned back. Looking back, you are amazed how a relationship that started with such high hopes and optimism has slowly turned into profound disappointment and disillusionment.

In the early years of married life, your desire for each other and romantic infatuation quickly spurred you on; there was traveling, visiting relatives, entertaining, outings and excursions, making new friends, and, of course, the excitement of conceiving new additions to the family. But all the adventures and excitement eventually came in a big circle back to square one, and you settled down to a boring routine. Like all things, the spark of fire finally came to an end. The reality of life has taken its toll. The two of you are busy trying to earn more money and keep up with the seemingly endless tasks of child care and home management. Slowly but steadily the bed has become a place only for sharing sleep, not intimacy. With the additions to the family, you now feel you are trapped in this hopeless and unbearably incompatible marriage that is doomed to failure. On the one hand, you suffer from sexual frustration and/or rejection and feel like terminating the marriage. On the other hand, you love your children and feel you should do something to salvage the marriage. You are at the crossroad.

Does this sound familiar? Every love story has a romantic beginning, but more than 50 percent of marriages end painfully in divorce. Marriage has an image problem. Read the statistics. Marriage rates are at historic lows, while the divorce rates are hitting record highs. Still, most people want to get married, and most do. And those who don't will be, or are, in some kind of committed sexual relationship, either as a prelude to marriage or an alternative to it.

Stable marriages are, and always have been, the cornerstone of every society. The importance people place on lasting and happy marriages is reflected in the wedding customs that have developed over the years. Since the wedding marks the beginning of marriage, it was thought important for the bride and groom not to fall prey to bad luck and evil spirits. As a result, an almost endless number of customs and superstitions accumulated. Many tend to be regional or culturally specific. Some are widely known and have become part of our traditions, such as the bride not being seen in her wedding dress by the groom before the ceremony. It was believed that it brought luck if the groom arrived at the church before the bride. The bride and groom cut the first slice of cake together to ensure they would conceive. The tradition of throwing rice (or birdseed or confetti) as the couple leaves the church dates back to ancient times and was meant to bestow fertility on the couple. Why do the bridesmaids dress so elegantly? This was designed to fool the evil spirits, so they would not know who the bride was.[1] Despite the fact that these are merely rituals and wishful ideals and even superstitions, they expressed—at least originally—the desire of everyone that the couple would live happily together ever after. And, indeed, many couples, especially from those older generations, did live happily ever after.

My mom and dad passed away some years ago. I admire them for staying happily married despite the ups and downs. I thank them for loving each other, for going through tough times together, and for surviving together till the end of life. They were simple people, and yet they were special and unique because they belonged to that very small group of people who reach their fiftieth wedding anniversary. I need only to look around my neighborhood today to feel proud of my parents. I am grateful I belonged to a very special group of kids whose parents lived together all their lives. This made my childhood much easier and simpler. I did not have more than one mother or more than one father. I did not have to deal with the conflicting (sometimes even unreasonable) demands of divorced or separated parents. I did not have to face the choice of who to live with. I did not have to sleep in different beds on different days of the week. I did not have to know anything about financial hardships. I played soccer, and I knew my mom or, sometimes, my dad would pick me up after the game. I did not have to worry about anything. I knew they loved me. I had two role models to look up to—a male and a female—even though they might not be as perfect as I wished. I was just a kid, as a kid should be. During my youth, divorce was a scary and shameful word, and divorce was rare news.

When people marry, they pledge before their friends, families, the state, the world, and in most cases their God (or gods) that they will remain faithful to one another until separated by death. Their vows imply mutual trust in each other's commitment to exclusive intimacy of their bodies, minds, and souls. They also imply exclusive sharing of many of the ups and downs in life. The word *exclusive* reminds us that there are certain feelings, knowledge, and experiences that belong to the couple alone, to the exclusion of others. It is as if there were a fence surrounding the relationship, marking off that which is exclusive to the husband and wife.

Times have changed. The lofty ideal of marriage largely has been replaced by modern negative images of marriage that have undermined marital stability and contributed to the breakdown of marriage as an institution. To some extent there is a misconception that marriage is good for men but bad for women—that it contributes wealth and well-being to males but makes women sick and unhappy. Often violence and abuse are portrayed as typical within marriage, and only Christians and some minority groups are seen as still favoring marriage despite its being an unjust, unsafe, and violent social arrangement. As the traditional family structure of husband, wife, and children gives way to other forms of family life, demographers and sociologists throughout the world are asking why.

To many, it now seems a natural thing to have a trial marriage. The argument is that one has to try it out first to ascertain whether a potential long-term mate is actually compatible and has similar tastes. Chastity is no more the norm. The media often report in great detail the glamorous, extravagant weddings of celebrities and, with equal detail, their divorces and remarriages. With the emerging trend of multiple marriages and divorces, which some coin "serial polygamy," the meaning of marriage itself has been stretched and distorted. In fact, the traditional definition of a family has been expanded to include all sorts of associations. So long as two willing, mature persons live under one roof, they are considered a couple and can be defined as a family.

Do all these practices and experimentations make for many happy "couples"? Apparently not. Divorce rates still remain high. Today a marriage certificate seems to be worth no more than the paper on which it is printed. The percentage of people reporting being "very happy" with their marriages has fallen from about 67 percent in 1970 to 62 percent in 2008.[2] Indeed, a close friend of mine puts it this way: "The marriage institution has broken down." And who suffers the most because of all this? The children, of course. Around one in four of them spend at least part of their childhood with only one parent. My neighbor's son one day told me he had to check with his friend to find out which home she would be in for the weekend before he could visit her. Her parents had divorced, and she lived with each of them on alternate weeks.

Times indeed have changed. Single parenthood has become a permanent and noticeable trend in many societies today. The U.S. Census Bureau reported that the number of single mothers in 2000 in U.S was ten million while single fathers numbered two million.[3] In Australia, the rise in single-parent households is primarily attributable to the rising rate of separations between parents.[4] In 2006, 22 percent of Australian families with children under the age of fifteen were single-parent families.[5] A staggering 87 percent of these families were headed by the mothers, while only 13 percent were headed by fathers. Most of these single mothers were middle-aged and previously married,[6] and they remain among the poorest segments of Australia's population.[7] In America, two-parent families have declined from 68 percent in 1970 to 42 percent in 2000.[8] The three main factors contributing to relationship difficulties cited in the Australian relationship survey are financial difficulties, work or study demands, and having or bringing up children.[9] Yes, that is correct—bringing up children.

The traditional concept of marriage and marital roles is being called into question—if not abandoned altogether—in this century more than ever before. The imbalance in the distribution of workloads at home and in earnings at the workplace are seen as compounding the inequality of the sexes and as discrimination against women. The husband's former role as leader, provider, and protector is rapidly diminishing. More and more females have entered the workforce to gain social and economic independence. The simple goal of getting married in order to establish a home, have children, and get ahead socially and economically has snowballed into a complex array of goals that may include friendship, support, fun, entertainment, personal growth, life fulfillment, social status, and financial stability.

With such a long list of goals for each partner, it is easy to get the priorities wrong and/or neglect certain important goals of one's partner. With all the temptations and distractions that go along with the ever-changing priorities, the chances of being sidetracked from achieving personal goals and those of our spouses are ever increasing as we journey through married life. It is pretty clear that while the number of options for marriage relationships has gone up, the satisfaction from marriage relationships has gone down. The introduction of no-fault divorce further fuels this trend, because it facilitates unilateral divorce.[10]

Largely because of these confusing and conflicting goals, the *soul-mate* model of marriage has overtaken the more traditional institutional model of marriage. In the soul-mate model, husbands and wives may share a home but not necessarily their lives. Marriage becomes a means of self-fulfillment, self-centered romance, and lust—a relationship based on convenience and mutual benefits (or exploitation). For example, I know a couple who married for the sake of social status and so they could share their expenses.

Yes, the concept of marriage is indeed changing. Traditionally, marriage signified the formation of a new family and the initiation of a sexual relationship. In the 1960s, traditional marriage was challenged by the practice of free love, mainly because the contraceptive pill became widely available. In the 1970s open marriage was the prevalent trend, as people married but agreed to permit extramarital affairs. By the 1980s, with the acceptance of cohabitation, formal marriage was on the decline. In the 1990s the 50-percent divorce rate was the norm in many developed countries. Finally, in the 2000s, the pluralization of the concepts of marriage gave rise to the complexity of the family unit. Many children today live with only a single biological parent, while many others grow up without ever knowing who their biological parents are. Some are adopted or fostered. Some live in blended family settings when a parent goes on to have children with a new partner, who may or may not have children from a previous relationship. And, sadly, some children live on the streets.

Some religious groups strongly encourage members to find their partners within their own religious affiliation, arguing that differences in religion can be a cause of marital unhappiness. However, in recent years, the religious barriers between denominations and religions have broken down. Hargrave[11] observes that religion seems to have become increasingly irrelevant to the choice of mates in modern secular society, even though rates of endogamous marriage still remain high.[12] This helps to explain why the divorce rates among secular and Christian marriages are not significantly different.

Statistics show that more and more people are unhappy despite all the diversity and choices of sexual lifestyles. Yet with all the daunting statistics stacked against a successful marriage, marriage still retains its powerful ideological significance.[13] It is true that more people are marrying later in life and more are practicing cohabitation before marriage, but according to the U.S. Census Bureau, about 90 percent of Americans will eventually marry.[14] People still see marriage as a worthy institution, so not all hope is lost. But we need to regain what *is* lost. We need to go back to the Bible to rediscover our identity and purpose in life and the purpose of marriage in God's plan.

Summary

The marriage *ceremony* is a human invention in which a man and a woman declare to their relatives and friends and to the world that they promise to live together as husband and wife for the rest of their lives. Although rituals and ceremonies have changed over time, the reasons for them remain the same: to express the couple's desire and the witnesses' wish that they live happily ever after. Their vows remind them of their mutual trust in each other's commitment to exclusive intimacy of their bodies, minds, and souls and to sharing the ups and downs of life.

The traditional concept of marriage largely has been replaced by the soul-mate model of marriage. The simple goal of getting married in order to live as husband and wife and have children has snowballed into a complex array of goals such as friendship, support, fun, entertainment, personal growth, life fulfillment, social status, and financial stability. The idea of "try before you buy" has caught the attention of many in the search for the perfect match, and chastity has been thrown out the window in the pursuit of lust and indulgence. The Hollywood style of multiple marriages and divorces is in fashion and often seen as the norm. And with the introduction of no-fault divorce, divorce rates have skyrocketed. The trend is clear: We are witnessing a total breakdown of marriage.

Divorce rates among Christians are not far behind the national averages. Yet this should not come as a surprise since the church tends to follow the models practiced by the wider community. This is why we desperately need to rediscover God's plan concerning marriage.

CHAPTER 2

Love: Obedience and Survival in Genesis 1

Be fruitful, and multiply, and fill the earth, and subdue it: and have dominion over the fish of the sea, and over the fowl of the air, and over every living thing that moves upon the earth.
Genesis 1:28

Many suggest that the message of the whole Bible is about love, and indeed this is so. It is about God's love for mankind, and that message appears in the first chapter of the Bible. The highlight of God's creation was the creation of humans. And herein is the first love. It is a love that is admired and reverenced by many; yet it is often little understood.

The first human beings appear in the first account of creation in Genesis 1, where God immediately commands them to be fruitful and multiply. The first human love story is recorded for us in Genesis 2 in the second account of creation. These two accounts of the same creation represent two aspects of marriage. The first, external to the garden, represents survival of the family and marriage through obedience to God's commands; the second, inside the garden, represents the intimate relationship between husband and wife, as reflected in their sacrifice and submission. Both ideas revolve around love, and in both aspects God stands at the center of the relationship.

The first creation account in Genesis 1 describes the chronological order of creation in six days. The climax of God's creative work is the creation of humans. There is no mention of the creation of the Garden of Eden and no mention of the entry of sin into the world.

The second creation account in Genesis 2 focuses solely on the creation of humans and the intimate relationship between Adam and Eve with God at their side. The creation of the garden is a means by which God shows his love to the first human beings.

Name of God: God

Even the name of God reflects the purpose of his creation. The word translated "God" throughout the chapter in Genesis 1 is *Elohim* (*el-o-heem'*) in Hebrew. This name implies the power of the almighty God. He is the uncreated, uncaused, self-existing one. He is the universal God, dignified and majestic. He is purposeful, patient, and powerful.

The style of the first creation account is measured and precise. We read about God separating light from darkness, water from dry land, and heaven from earth. God was establishing boundaries that would ensure the survival of the creation. God saw these boundaries as good. One of the greatest challenges for humanity has been to acknowledge that God's boundaries are not hindrances but are, in fact, good.

God created everything by his Word; he spoke, and "it was so." The Bible identifies Jesus as the Word.

> *In the beginning was the Word, and the Word was with God, and the Word was God. The same was in the beginning with God. All things were made by him; and without him was not any thing made that was made. . . . And the Word was made flesh, and dwelt among us.*
> *John 1:1-3, 14*

Jesus obeyed God the Father and created all things.

Jesus, our Creator, set many examples for us to follow, and his teachings are powerful. We learn in Luke 4:1–13 that Satan tempted Jesus in the wilderness, but Jesus resisted the temptations by quoting the Scriptures. Satan likewise tempts us, and one of his most successful tactics is establishing strongholds in our lives. These are things that hinder our spiritual growth, cause frustration and friction between husbands and wives, and even break up families. These strongholds can be such things as ambitions, hobbies, work, or wealth. These things may be fine in themselves, but when they become so important to us that we are willing to exceed the boundaries God has established for us and disobey God, we fall prey to Satan's devious schemes; and we and our families suffer as a result.

In Mathew 19:16–24, a youth asked Jesus how he could obtain eternal life. When Jesus replied, "Go and sell what you have, and give to the poor, and you shall have treasure in heaven: and come and follow me," the young man went away sorrowful. Jesus knew this man's possessions were his stronghold, and unless he was willing to abandon them, he could not have a proper relationship with God. Having a proper relationship with God, obeying his commands and accepting his good boundaries, insulates us against breakdown in our marriage and family.

Creation of Humans

The creation of human beings represents the climax of all creation. God created the heavens, earth, light, darkness, plants, fishes, birds, and animals, but the creation of humans as *male and female* was the ultimate creative achievement of God.

> *And God said, Let us make man in our image, after our likeness: and let them have dominion over the fish of the sea, and over the fowl of the air, and over the cattle, and over all the earth, and over every creeping thing that creeps upon the earth. So God created man in his own image, in the image of God created he him; male and female created he them. And God blessed them, and God said unto them, Be fruitful, and multiply, and fill the earth, and subdue it: and have dominion over the fish of the sea, and over the fowl of the air, and over every living thing that moves upon the earth.*
> *Genesis 1:26–28*

Although there is a temporal, sequential order in the creation of humans—first male and then female—the narrative in Genesis 1 describes the creation of human beings in one majestic stroke of the pen. It gives no details of the differences in the creation of male and female. God simply made *man* (singular) but refers to *man* as *them* (plural). The same style occurs in verse 27. These apparent grammatical anomalies reflect the fact that *man* is used as a generic term for *human beings* and encompasses both male and female. This is confirmed in Genesis 5:2,

Love: Obedience and Survival

where *Adam* (the Hebrew word for *man* used in Genesis 1:26–27) refers to both *male and female*[i].

Male and female created he them; and blessed them, and called their name Adam, in the day when they were created.
Genesis 5:2

Clearly, then, both male and female are created in the image of God.

This plural nature of male-female designation as God's image may seem strange. Various explanations have been offered. However, in the context of Genesis 1:26, where God is described using the plural pronouns ("let *us*"; "in *our* likeness"), it suggests the multi-personality of God. This plural nature is reflected in his creation of human beings. God is neither male nor female. He transcends both genders.

Survival and Male and Female Roles

God then gave man a series of commands that were designed to ensure the survival of the human race. The first of these commands was to reproduce and populate the earth. The rest of the commands concern man's subduing and taking dominion over other life-forms. Again, this is about life and life-supporting activities. Here, the commands apply

---

[i] The *female* apparently acquired the name Eve only after the fall (Gen 3:20); that is, after they were cast out of the garden.

equally to both male and female. This is important to note, for it shows that in the eyes of God, male and female are equal, even though there is a temporal order in their creation.

God wants women, not just men, to have dominance over the earth and manage all things. We are given the task of managing this world—the water, the aquatic environment, the air, the climate, every plant and animal, and all matter under the sun. This is quite contrary to the general status of women throughout history and even into modern times. Evidence abounds that women often have been denied equality in almost every level of society and every culture throughout the ages, yet the Bible gives prominence to many women. Some put the number of named women in the Bible at 188.[15] In the Old Testament, we have the midwives Shiphrah and Puah (Exodus 1:15), the prophetess and judge Deborah (Judges 4:4), Miriam (Exodus 15:20), and others. We have a whole book written about the famous "wherever-you-go" daughter-in-law Ruth and another about Esther, the great heroine of the Jews. In the New Testament, we have Phoebe the deaconess, Persis, Lois, Eunice, Julia, and others (Romans 16:1–15)—all women disciples who were working very hard for God. There are also a number of great women leaders such as Tabitha, Lydia, and Priscilla. In fact, it was Priscilla, along with her husband Aquila, who taught the gospel to Apollos (Acts 18:26).

A cursory study of the attitude Jesus had toward the women in his life reveals, not condescension or apathy, but respect and love in equal measure to their male counterparts. Anna was the prophetess who recognized the baby Jesus as the coming one the Jews were looking for (Luke 2:36–38). Mary of Bethany anointed Jesus at a banquet served by her sister Martha (John 12:1–3). It was a group of women who embarked on the journey to the tomb and discovered and first reported the resurrection of Christ Jesus, even though women were not considered reliable witnesses at that time. Women are not inferior in the sight of God. Even though societies and practices may be biased in favor of males, the Bible gives credit where credit is deserved. It commends and honors women in both the Old and New Testaments.

The oracle of King Lemuel summarizes the biblical roles of women in society very elegantly.

> *She is like the merchants' ships; she brings her food from afar. She rises also while it is yet night, and gives food to her household, and a portion to her maidservants. She considers a field, and buys it: with the fruit of her hands she plants a vineyard. She girds her loins with strength, and strengthens her arms. She perceives that her merchandise is good: her lamp goes not out by night. She lays her hands to the distaff, and her hands hold the spindle. She stretches out her hand to the poor; yea, she reaches forth her hands to the needy. She is not afraid of the snow for her household: for all her household are clothed with scarlet. She makes herself coverings of tapestry; her clothing is fine linen and purple. Her husband is known in the gates, when he sits among the elders of the land.*

She makes fine linen, and sells it; and delivers sashes unto the merchants. Strength and honor are her clothing; and she shall rejoice in time to come. She opens her mouth with wisdom; and on her tongue is the law of kindness. She looks well to the ways of her household, and eats not the bread of idleness.
Proverbs 31:14–27

Much like her male counterpart, the woman described in these verses is independent and in control in daily activities. She makes many decisions independently of her husband. She buys and sells properties and merchandise. She runs a business. She manages the household. She is a breadwinner, she engages in commercial activities, managing the budgets and finances, and she gives instructions as one in authority. This description reminds me of Abigail, the wife of Nabal, who overrode the poor decision of her husband by ordering his servants to provide food and drink for David, who was on the run from King Saul (1 Samuel 25:10–19).

The garden described in Genesis 2 was private to Adam and Eve. There was no immediate need for procreation, for the environment was protected and secure. There was plenty of food, no cooking to do, no washing of clothes, and no laborious work. However, once Adam and Eve were driven from the garden because of their disobedience, they faced a very hostile environment, and for the first time the Bible records that Eve gave birth to children. God foresaw this and issued the command to the first couple to "be fruitful and multiply." Survival of the human race depended on Adam and Eve's obedience to this command.

All other living creatures were divinely endowed with the instinct to reproduce.

> *And God said, Let the earth bring forth living creatures after their kinds, cattle, and creeping things, and beasts of the earth after their kinds: and it was so.*
> *Genesis 1:24*

All creatures, as well as the human race, survive through sexual reproduction. Thus, sex is designed for reproduction and survival.

The only distinction Genesis 1 makes between the creation of humans and other living things is that humans are created in God's image. By virtue of bearing God's image, humans are assigned the task of exercising some of his authority to rule over the earth and all other living things. Humans assume the authority of God's agents.

The mandate to reproduce was designed to ensure the survival of the human race. The mandate does not differentiate between males and females, implying that it is not for one sex to dominate the other. Rather, through their harmonious union and cooperation, males and females fulfill God's command to ensure human dominion and control over his creation. Although there is sexual differentiation of humans into male and female, maleness or femaleness plays no role in the dominion humans are to have over God's creation. The Scriptures give no hint of a division of responsibilities or of a distinction of rank in their administration of this mandate. The mandate to rule applies equally to both males and females, and the command is given to both.

> *Subdue it: and have dominion over the fish of the sea, and over the fowl of the air, and over every living thing that moves upon the earth.*
> *Genesis 1:28*

After the fall of Adam and Eve, there were additional responsibilities to ensure the survival of the human race. Adam was to toil in his labor, while Eve was primarily responsible for childbearing. Quite distinct from the mandate to control and manage God's creation, where both male and female have equal responsibilities, here we see a division, or sharing, of responsibilities for the care and maintenance of a family. The question is this: How do we share these responsibilities? In olden days, the family roles and tasks were devised to meet the conditions of hunting and agricultural societies, so this was pretty straightforward: The husband did the physical labor, and the wife tended to housekeeping chores.

However, the situation has changed. Despite the aid of modern appliances such as vacuum cleaners, washing machines, refrigerators, and dishwashers, housework has actually increased. Child care and child education and all that go with them are now more demanding than ever. Outdoor chores are also time-consuming. As the standard of living goes up, so does the cost of living. Dual-income households are common nowadays, as the wife has to supplement the family income in order to meet the rising costs of living. As societies have moved away from hunting and agriculture, women have been given more opportunities to earn a living. In some instances, they are the primary breadwinners of their families.

As a result of all these social changes, the roles and responsibilities of a household have become blurred. Among the many proposals for what should be the responsibilities and roles of husbands and wives are the following.

The husband should be the breadwinner.

The husband should provide leadership and make major decisions.

The wife should be the primary child-care provider and take care of the house.

The wife's job or career is equally important to the husband's.

The husband should share an equal amount of household chores.

The wife should be in charge of household finances and budgets.

Husband and wife should consult one another before making important decisions.

The husband should always have the final say.

Expenses should be shared equally.

Husband and wife should cooperate and find out who does what best.

Husband and wife should be honest with one another.

Each spouse should be considerate of the needs of the other.

Husband and wife should take turns with various chores.

The wife should be obedient.

Couples must stop the blame game.

Couples should stop weighing who has done more today and who has done less.

Before marriage, couples should have a discussion of their roles and responsibilities.

It is important to adopt a positive attitude toward conflicts between work and family life.

Couples should have a prenuptial agreement.

Care should be taken to avoid overloading "unpopular" jobs on one person.

The list goes on and on. But where do we turn when confronted with all these ideas, many of which conflict with one another?

When we look to the Bible, we find many detailed laws relating to various aspects of life. Nowhere is this more evident than in the Mosaic laws. Those laws regulated the Jewish priesthood, sacrifices, rituals, and offerings, which foreshadowed the ultimate sacrifice of Jesus on the cross. There were hundreds of laws, and they were a great burden for the people to adhere to; and, in fact, the people consistently failed to obey them. An endless list of laws or rules, it seems, will only prove how incapable we are of keeping them.

How about the Ten Commandments? There are only ten of them. One might think they would be simple to keep. Well, the Bible tells us that we all fail to keep those commandments as well. Indeed, a glance at the crime statistics of any country shows how prone people are to failing to comply with both God's and man's laws. It is no surprise, then, that there are conflicts between husbands and wives over various issues, ranging from household chores to gardening, to vacations, to finance, to child care, and even to choices of meals and clothing, and sleeping habits. But how do we resolve these issues? We get married to enjoy life together, to be united as one, and to bear the yoke together, not to be burdened with more rules. Wouldn't it be nice to have just a handful of easy and simple rules to follow? Yes; and, thank God, there is.

> *Jesus said unto him, You shall love the Lord your God with all your heart, and with all your soul, and with all your mind. This is the first and great commandment. And the second is like unto it, You shall love your neighbor as yourself. On these two commandments hang all the law and the prophets.*
> *Matthew 22:37–40*

To understand how these two commandments relate to marriage, we need to go back to the origin of the Ten Commandments and establish the connection between the old Ten Commandments and the love commandments in Mathew 22.

There are various ideas today about the Ten Commandments. Some teach they are done away with and those who seek to keep them are practicing a form of legalism. Various Scriptures, such as the book of Galatians, are cited to prove this. However, a careful examination of Galatians shows that the issues it is addressing are circumcision and justification by faith. A careful look at some other Scriptures will confirm that the Ten Commandments are a necessary part of the code of conduct we all must strive to live by. The Ten Commandments are like a mirror that shows us who we actually are and what state we are in. They cannot rectify our state. Rather, they act as a standard by which we measure our performance. They are recognized as the moral foundations of Judaism and Christianity. The Ten Commandments appear twice in the Bible—once in Exodus 20 and a second time in Deuteronomy 5—and they are referred to throughout the Bible. Even the last chapter of the last book of the Bible speaks of the commandments.

> *Blessed are they that do his commandments, that they may have right to the tree of life, and may enter in through the gates into the city. For outside are dogs, and sorcerers, and fornicators, and*

> *murderers, and idolaters, and whosoever loves and makes a lie.*
> *Revelation 22:14–15*

Jesus referred to the Ten Commandments on several occasions, and he had this to say to us.

> *If you keep my commandments, you shall abide in my love; even as I have kept my Father's commandments, and abide in his love.*
> *John 15:10*

Jesus obeyed the Father's commandments, and he asks us to demonstrate our love for him by obeying his two commandments. However, we must not think that Jesus has substituted his commandments for his Father's commandments or that the Ten Commandments are abolished. Jesus taught his disciples that he came not to destroy the law or the prophets but to fulfill them (Matthew 5:17). The law and the prophets refer to all the laws of the Old Testament, including the Ten Commandments. He encourages us to keep these laws (Matthew 5:19).

> *Think not that I am come to destroy the law, or the prophets: I am not come to destroy, but to fulfill. For verily I say unto you, Till heaven and earth pass away, one jot or one tittle shall in no wise pass from the law, till all be fulfilled. Whosoever therefore shall break one of these least commandments, and shall teach men so, he shall be called the least in the kingdom of heaven: but*

> *whosoever shall do and teach them, the same shall be called great in the kingdom of heaven.*
> *Matthew 5:17–19*

Consider this hypothetical example. A man breaks a law, and the judge orders him either to go to jail for one month or pay a fine. If he cannot afford to pay the fine he will, of course, go to jail. But a good Samaritan comes along and pays the fine for him. The judge then sets him free because the law has been satisfied, or fulfilled. The law is not destroyed; it is still in effect. If, after this, the man breaks the law again, the judge certainly will hand down an even more severe judgment against him.

Jesus has done the hard work for us by bearing the punishment due for our sins, thus fulfilling the requirements of breaking the Ten Commandments. In return, he wants us to keep his commandments: love God and love our neighbor. God's commandments are not abolished. That is why the apostle Paul queries the wisdom of continuing to break the commandments.

> *What shall we say then? Shall we continue in sin, that grace may abound? God forbid. How shall we, that are dead to sin, live any longer in it?*
> *Romans 6:1–2*

Jesus has revealed the means by which we can keep the Ten Commandments. If we love our parents, we will be proud of them and honor them; we will not curse them or do things that disgrace them. Neither will we be disobedient to them. If we love our fellow human beings, we will not do anything that may harm them; we will not steal their belongings or kill them. Wouldn't it be a better place to live if we practiced LOVE? It is much easier to keep the two love commandments than the Ten Commandments. However, we can still look to the Ten Commandments as a measure of our obedience to God.

The Ten Commandments and Marriage

The love commandments have their origin in the Old Testament. The books of the Law—Genesis, Exodus, Leviticus, Numbers, and Deuteronomy—are built on the principle of love.

> *And you shall love the LORD your God with all your heart, and with all your soul, and with all your might.*
> *Deuteronomy 6:5*

The first four of the Ten Commandments relate to God.

I am the Lord your God, and you shall not have other gods besides me.

You shall not make any graven image for yourself.

You shall not take the name of the Lord your God in vain (i.e., blasphemy).

Remember the Lord's Day to keep it holy (i.e., six days working and one day reserved for God).

These commandments address man's relationship with God. God is to be the sole object of our worship. His name is to be revered. We must not make ourselves greater than God or claim to be God or engage in blasphemous activities. And the Sabbath is to be a sign that God is the Creator and that we are his special creation.

By loving God as Jesus commanded, we inevitably fulfill the obligations of these four commandments. If we love God, we will not worship other idols. If we love God, we will not place ourselves or anything else above God. If we love God, we will want to worship him and glorify his name. We will want to do things that please him. He will be the focus of our lives.

When a husband and wife have the same focus and the same love for God, they will naturally have many things in common. Their aspirations in life—careers, business dealings, home chores, responsibilities toward one another and their children, financial considerations, entertainment—will all be weighed and valued in terms of their love for God. Finding the common denominator when there is a conflict certainly will be much easier. In fact, the couple will be on a convergent course in life, riding toward the sunset in life together. Of course, this does not guarantee that Christian couples will have a perfectly happy married life. However, the chances of having a happy marriage certainly increase exponentially as the couple walk together in life. Indeed, the main criterion for a happy marriage is truly loving God.

I remember when I first became aware of Christianity during high school. A friend invited me to his home. There was a sign there that read: "The Lord Jesus is the head of this home." Sadly, in observing the family's behavior, I concluded that their love of God was wanting. Like so many Christians, they failed to fully obey God's commands. No wonder the divorce rate of Christian couples is only slightly lower than that of non-Christians.

Loving God encourages us to be more positive and proactively engage in activities that show our obedience to God and our willingness to please him. The first three of the Ten Commandments teach us NOT to commit certain wrongs, or sins. Yet, we are like children who tend to rebel against the "laws" set by their parents. I recall soldering a broken circuit board as my young son watched. I showed him how hot it was by touching the soldering iron on a lead flux so that it gave out smoke. I told him it was very hot and told him not to touch it. I put away the iron inside a protective soldering iron holder and walked to the next room to get something. Within seconds I heard a loud cry. As you might have guessed, he had already pulled out the iron and touched the rod. Aren't we very much like that when it comes to God's commands?

The fourth commandment requires us to set aside one day per week as holy. We are to rest on this day, putting aside all worldly things and focusing on holy things. At least once a week, as husband and wife we are to gather together in holy communion with God. This is not just about going to church and worshiping; it is also about replenishing and reinforcing the relationship between husband and wife. There is a direct relationship between the husband and wife on the one hand and God and the church on the other hand. As the bond between the family and God increases, so the bond between husband and wife is strengthened.

The last six commandments relate to our fellow humans.

Honor your father and your mother.

You shall not kill.

You shall not commit adultery.

You shall not steal.

You shall not bear false witness.

You shall not covet your neighbor's house, you shall not covet your neighbor's wife, . . . nor any thing that is your neighbor's.

Jesus aptly summarizes these six commandments into just one: "Love your neighbor." Again, he was quoting a verse in the Old Testament.

> *You shall love your neighbor as yourself: I am the LORD.*
> *Leviticus 19:18*

A neighbor is anyone other than ourselves. If we were all willing to abide by these six commandments, our society would be a safer, more caring, and happy community. We would honor our parents and parents-in-law. We would not covet what someone else possesses, and crime rates would drop. When we truly love our neighbors, we do our part to make the world a better place, and we find our own life fulfilling.

Let us not forget that God loves humanity deeply and desires that every human being obey his commandments for their good and for his glory. Obedience is certainly the expectation for Christians and for Christian couples, who may properly view their spouses as their "neighbors." Of course, Paul goes much further than that, saying men should "love their wives as their own bodies" (Ephesians 5:28)! Doesn't that sound romantic?

Summary

Genesis presents one and only one creation, although there are two accounts of it. The first account gives few details about the creation of man but rather emphasizes God's initial commands to man. First, God commanded man—male and female—to multiply. Thus, Genesis 1 stresses the reproductive purpose of sex. Second, God commanded humans to have dominance over all his creation because they alone are created in his image. Indeed, men and women are managers of God's creation and are responsible to him as his agents. Obedience to these two commands was necessary for the survival of the race, especially in the hostile environment man would face outside the Garden of Eden.

For society to function properly, however, God also gave us the Ten Commandments. Jesus summarized the Ten Commandments in the two love commandments that had long been hidden away in the Old Testament: Love God and love our neighbor. These love commandments form the foundation upon which a happy marriage can be built. Couples who obey these commands will assure the survival and prosperity of their marriages, for those who love God and love others as they love themselves will protect and help each other as God intended.

CHAPTER 3

Love: Sacrifice and Submission in Genesis 2

Therefore shall a man leave his father and his mother, and shall cleave unto his wife: and they shall be one flesh.
Genesis 2:24

The second account of creation in Genesis 2 is about a love relationship. It is, in fact, a love story—a love story God wants us to experience. God's creation is centered on humans and his plan for us to survive, to manage and control his creation, to love other humans, to love our spouses, and to love him.

In the Genesis 1 account, God emphasized the command to man—both male and female—to be fruitful and multiply in the earth. This command was to ensure the survival of the human race. Adam and Eve eventually disobeyed God and consequently were expelled from the garden. However, they certainly obeyed the command to multiply! Our world population has currently reached 6.9 billion and is estimated to reach around 9 billion by 2040.[16] Genesis 1, then, stresses the reproductive aspect of sex for the survival of the human race. And, as we have seen, it also underscores the equality of men and women.

The second creation account focuses on the creation of humans and the garden for humans to live in. Whereas the first account sets forth the chronological order of the creation of all things, the account in Genesis 2 focuses specifically on the creation of humans and their immediate environment. This shift is marked by the word *generations* in Genesis 2:4.

> *These are the generations of the heavens and of the earth when they were created, in the day that the LORD God made the earth and the heavens*
> *Genesis 2:4*

In the book of Genesis the phrase "These are the generations of " appears repeatedly. "Generations" is the translation of the Hebrew *toledah* (*to-led-aw'*), denoting a family history or successions.[17] This same word appears again in relation to Adam's line (5:1–6:8), Noah's family (6:9–9:29), Noah's sons (10:1–11:9), Shem's line (11:10–26), Terah and Abram's families (11:27–25:11), and in other places—altogether eleven times in Genesis. Each time the phrase appears, it introduces a new section of the book. Here in Genesis 2:4, it introduces a change from the general account of creation that preceded it to the specific account of the creation and subsequent history of the family of Adam.

Again, the two creation accounts in Genesis are not accounts of two different creations. Nor are there any contradictions in the creation stories of Genesis 1 and Genesis 2. Rather, these are two narratives of the same creation from two different perspectives

In Genesis 2, the author steps back from the temporal sequence of creation to the sixth day and reveals more details of the creation of man as male and female. The account shows the gentler, more intimate, and anthropomorphic sides of God, as he reveals his love plan for humanity and the establishment of the first love with the creation of Adam and Eve. First, God, who is identified by his personal name, Jehovah (*yeh-ho-vaw'*), creates the garden to cater to the special needs of the new couple. We see that the man takes charge and calls the animals by names. Unlike the creation of other creatures, human male and female are closely bonded by the fact that the female is created out of a rib of the man and that the man "will leave his father and mother and be united to his wife, and they will become one flesh" (Genesis 2:24 NIV).

The Order of Creation

Unlike in Genesis 1, God's commands in Genesis 2 are directed *through* Adam, and he expects both Adam and Eve to obey them.

> *And the LORD God commanded the man, saying, Of every tree of the garden you may freely eat: But of the tree of the knowledge of good and evil, you shall not eat of it: for in the day that you eat thereof you shall surely die. . . . And out of the ground the LORD God formed every beast of the field, and every fowl of the air; and brought them unto Adam to see what he would call them: and whatsoever Adam called every living creature, that was its name.*
> *Genesis 2:16-17, 19*

At this point in time, Eve did not yet exist. The commands were issued to Adam, and when Eve came along, she had to trust Adam and obey the commands as Adam told her. In other words, Adam took the lead, and Eve followed. This seems to suggest an inequality of *roles,* in contrast to the principle laid down in Genesis 1. Paul emphasizes these role differences and explains in 1 Timothy 2:13, "For Adam was formed first, then Eve." Indeed, in Genesis 2 the male is created first, followed by the creation of the female.

> *And the LORD God formed man of the dust of the ground, and breathed into his nostrils the breath of life; and man became a living soul. . . . And the LORD God caused a deep sleep to fall upon Adam, and he slept: and he took one of his ribs, and closed up its place with flesh; And from the rib, which the LORD God had taken from man, made he a woman.*
> *Genesis 2:7, 21–22*

We must remember that the establishment of the love relationship is in view here. God created a garden to provide the appropriate environment for love expressions and to exclude others from the relationship. Genesis 2 is about love and relationships, and God delegates different roles for male and female in that relationship, based on the order of their creation; and man was created first. This is not an issue of superiority. It is an issue of man being given a special role (and the accompanying responsibilities) in the love relationship. God created the man first in order to establish his leadership in the love relationship. We have not discussed in detail what this leadership role is about—that will be left for subsequent chapters. However, there is a need for leadership in any relationship. The leadership role as established by God, however, is not measured by one's intellect or abilities; it is established merely on the fact that Adam was created before Eve.

We must not confuse the issue here, which revolves around *human* relationships. The fact that *animals* were created before man in Genesis 1 does not suggest a dominant role for them over human beings. In fact, just the opposite is the case: Man was told to take dominion over the animal kingdom. The leadership role of the man, because his creation preceded that of the woman, is analogous to the prominence of the firstborn in Hebrew society. The firstborn in a Hebrew family had special privileges and responsibilities, simply because he was the firstborn. It never entered their minds that these privileges and responsibilities would be nullified if the father happened to own cattle before he had sons, because they would never lump animals and humans together as equal candidates for the role of *firstborn.*

In a family setting, the children do not have a say in whether they are born first, second, third, etc. They must simply accept their birth order. I was brought up in a family where the younger siblings respected the elder brothers and sisters. I happened to be the eldest, and I commanded the respect of my siblings without ever having to prove myself more intelligent or capable than they were. In return, both consciously and unconsciously, I was expected to protect and take care of them. I recall taking the bus to school every day with my younger brother. I was entrusted to pay the bus fares for both of us. Though my younger brother certainly could have paid his own bus fare, that was the arrangement. Of course, different families have different practices, but in general, even today, the eldest in the family is expected to lead.

I took the lead, together with its responsibility, without asking why. It just seemed the natural and expected thing. My brothers and sister respect me, even today, not necessarily because I deserve their respect, but because I am the eldest. We just graciously accept this order. We never think that there exists some inequality in our relationship because of this. I think the reason we never think this is because we are bonded by blood and bonded by love.

The same applies to my son and daughter. At times they might argue and quarrel, but they have never fought or complained over who was the firstborn, even when the oldest, my son, received special privileges (and responsibilities) above his younger sister. The point I am driving home is that when people are bound together by blood and by love, there is no such thing as inequality. Yes, we need a leader, and there can be just one. But that is not inequality, for it does not give greater value to one over another; it simply gives different responsibilities to the different parties.

Of course, in discussions about the husband-and-wife relationship, especially in this modern age, the matter of gender equality/inequality seems to always come to the forefront. However, we are called simply to accept the order laid down by God. Paul pointed out that the order is for the husband to lead because Adam was created first. Whether the husband or the wife is the more intelligent one is irrelevant. In a love relationship, God wants the husband to lead. It is the love bond that counts. Within that love bond, symbolized by the boundary of the Garden of Eden, God's plan is for the husband to take the lead. Superiority and equality are not issues.

I remember during a Bible study, a young Christian asked a very logical question: Why did not God create male and female simultaneously from the same lump of clay? Would that not have established their equality of personhood more clearly? The fact is God already had established their equality beyond any doubt in Genesis 1:27, where the Bible tells us both were created in God's image. We have seen that for survival and day-to-day activities, this equality means that men and women may engage in all sorts of activities with no restrictions whatsoever. Today, this may mean both husband and wife work to earn a comfortable living, or it could mean only the husband works while the wife takes care of the family. It may also be possible for the wife to work while the husband takes care of the family. However, when it comes to love and sexual relationships, God wants the husband to play the leadership role.

Name of God: LORD God

The name for the Creator used throughout Genesis 1 is simply "God," or *Elohim* (*el-o-heem'*) in Hebrew, which is the plural form of *El*, meaning God the almighty. The Genesis 2 creation account refers to the

Creator as "Lord God," (*yeh-ho-vaw' el-o-heem'*), which is the personal name of God. He is a personal God, the nationalistic God, in direct touch with his creation. The style in chapter 2 is a more personal, storytelling approach. This shows the intimate and loving personal nature of God. Thus the names set the tone of the two accounts of the one creation—the first stressing obedience and thus survival through reproduction, and the second emphasizing the love relationship.

The Creation Revisited

The LORD God planted a garden eastward in Eden, and there he put the man whom he had formed. . . . And the LORD God caused a deep sleep to fall upon Adam, and he slept: and he took one of his ribs, and closed up its place with flesh; And from the rib, which the LORD God had taken from man, made he a woman, and brought her unto the man.
Genesis 2:8, 21–22

Central to the second account of creation is the Garden in Eden. The Hebrew word *eden* (*ay'-den*) means delicate, pleasure, or delight. The garden was God's masterpiece. It was a place where God's desire for a relationship with humanity was expressed. It also was the place where intimate human relationships originated. Isaiah 51:3 describes it as the "Garden of the LORD," filled with joy and gladness, thanksgiving, and the voice of melody.

Love: Sacrifice and Submission

When my son was born, we bought him a wooden cot in which he could play and entertain himself and often sleep. We wanted to confine and protect him. We put some toys inside and made him as comfortable as possible. We made sure there were no sharp edges that might hurt him. We expressed how very much we loved him in these ways. In fact, before he was born, we had already planned all these things. The wooden cot created a boundary of protection that implicitly said, "Do not go outside; play inside the cot." As the child grew, we provided him with a bigger area in which to crawl about, and we put away from him things that might harm him, such as matches, knives, and items with small parts. We also started to tell him, using words and gestures he could understand, what he could and could not do.

Similarly, God created the garden and put Adam and Eve inside. He surrounded them with good things—animals, birds, and plants—and provided them with food. The boundary of the garden protected them and was one way God demonstrated his love for them. Later, when Adam and Eve were outside the garden, God showed his love for them by providing guidance to them and later to their descendants. Through Moses, God gave the Ten Commandments and the various laws. We learned that Jesus condensed the Ten Commandments into two (the commandments of love), which are about loving God and loving our fellow humans.

Love is a dynamic relationship. It is not static or stagnant. The fellow human closest to us, of course, is our spouse. In God's plan—and in the natural desire of humans—the husband loves his wife, and his wife reciprocates. Similarly, God loves us, and we also need to respond to his love. Indeed, Scripture spells out a clear relationship between God's divine, intimate love for his church (that is, Christians, who believe in Jesus) and the love between a husband and wife. By his intention, the intimate relationship between husband and wife is to reflect the love relationship between God (Christ) and his church (Ephesians 5:25–33).

It is remarkable that when Adam existed in a perfect world in perfect communion with his Creator, God saw that he was still not complete. "It is not good for the man to be alone," God said (Genesis 2:28 NIV). So God decided to make a helper suitable for him. However, God did not proceed immediately to create Eve for Adam. Instead, he brought a parade of animals before Adam for him to name. Why the delay? God wanted to prepare Adam for what was to come. In order to give the animals appropriate names, Adam had to study them and pay attention to their nature. In doing so, he doubtless noticed that there were male and female animals. We know from Genesis 3 that God talked to Adam, so it is quite possible God taught Adam all about the anatomy of these creatures. And with God as his teacher, Adam no doubt also acquired full knowledge of his own anatomy. The only thing lacking was a partner corresponding to him, because up to this point, Adam lived alone and without a female counterpart.

> *But for Adam there was not found a helper suitable for him.*

Genesis 2:20

After much delay, God finally created Eve.

God did not create Adam and Eve out of nothing, as he had created the heavens and the earth. God first formed, or molded (*yaw-tsar*), Adam out of the dust of the ground (Genesis 2:7), the way he had created the various creatures (verse 19). The creation of Eve was quite different. God took a rib out of Adam and made, or built or transformed (*baw-naw'*), it into a woman. In fact, the word *woman* means "from man." Molding a lump of clay into a man emphasizes that the man is an earthly being, made out of matter. Transforming the rib of a man into a female emphasizes the oneness and intimate relationship of the couple. From the very beginning, God sanctioned the sexual union of a man and a woman in marriage. The two were originally one, and in the holy union of the male and female, they become one flesh again. Jesus emphasizes this point when he says in Matthew 19:6, "What therefore God has joined together, let not man put asunder." Becoming one flesh is a holy act and is for life.

The Bible says that after creating Eve, God "brought her unto him [Adam]." Wasn't that wonderful? God did not force Adam and/or Eve to be joined together. Rather, God introduced her to him. And it was God who brought the bride to the bridegroom. Adam would have time to make his decision as to whether he wanted her as his bride. Similarly, Eve would have time to determine whether to accept or turn down

Adam. Here, we witness two consensual adults willing to tie the knot. This is the first divine marriage.

When God created Eve and brought her to Adam, the Bible says,

> *And Adam said, This is now bone of my bones, and flesh of my flesh: she shall be called Woman, because she was taken out of Man. Therefore shall a man leave his father and his mother, and shall cleave unto his wife: and they shall be one flesh. Genesis 2:23–24*

The sexual union of a male and a female makes them husband and wife, and in the eyes of God they are one flesh. God has made an end to two individual lives and has now made the man and woman, a one-flesh entity. God no longer sees them as two but as one. The presence of God almighty as the third-party witness to the marriage covenant makes it a lifetime commitment between the husband and the wife. The modern-day ceremonial performance by the minister or the magistrate is nothing more than the sanction of the church or the state on the real marriage. Just as baptism is the symbol of the real baptism by the Holy Spirit, the ceremonial marriage is merely a symbolic recognition of the real thing, when a couple first join together in sexual union. It is at that point they are bound together as one. Ideally, they are bound not only physically but also by real love that has its origin in the Lord, and their thoughts and affections coalesce, and the bond between them grows as the years go by. Yet, even if the ideal is absent, they are still bound. This is why Jesus cautions us not to divorce: we may be engaging in adulterous behavior.

> *Whosoever shall put away his wife, except it be for fornication, and shall marry another, commits adultery.*
> *Matthew 19:9*

The biblical definition of adultery is very different from those we find in our modern dictionaries, which merely reflect contemporary semantics and common ideas. In the eyes of God, a male and a female are married once they have a sexual relationship. Thus, a couple that is cohabiting is considered married, even if they have not legally married. There is no such thing as trial marriage. If they later join with different persons, they commit adultery. If one divorces in order to marry another, then he or she commits adultery.

Marriage, as God intended it, however, is not merely about the physical bonding of persons; it is also about the bonding of souls and spirits. Indeed, those who hop from one partner to the next miss out altogether on the joy of real love.

At this point in time, the relationship between God and Adam was close and intimate. Adam could talk with God and listen to his voice without worries or fears. However, as we will learn, once Adam sinned, this relationship was severed. The ability to comprehend God intimately was lost. However, not everything was lost, for God had a great master plan to restore the severed relationship and bring humanity back into intimate fellowship with him.

The Plot

> *Now the serpent was more subtle than any beast of the field which the LORD God had made. And he said unto the woman, Yea, has God said, you shall not eat of every tree of the garden? And the woman said unto the serpent, We may eat of the fruit of the trees of the garden: But of the fruit of the tree which is in the midst of the garden, God has said, You shall not eat of it, neither shall you touch it, lest you die. And the serpent said unto the woman, You shall not surely die: For God does know that in the day you eat thereof, then your eyes shall be opened, and you shall be as gods, knowing good and evil. And when the woman saw that the tree was good for food, and that it was pleasant to the eyes, and a tree to be desired to make one wise, she took of the fruit thereof, and did eat, and gave also unto her husband with her; and he did eat.*
> *Genesis 3:1–6*

There is much discussion and confusion about whether the storyline concerning the serpent in Genesis 3 should be taken literally or figuratively. Is it a real serpent or merely a symbolic representation of Satan? There is nothing to suggest the story is anything but real history; however, the details do raise questions. In his work, *The Antiquities of the Jews,* the ancient Jewish historian Flavius Josephus suggested that all the beasts in Genesis 3 spoke the same language, but after Adam and Eve were chased out of the garden, they spoke different languages. If they indeed spoke one language, this would explain how Satan, in the form of the serpent, was able to speak to Eve directly. Whatever the case actually was, the serpent did in fact communicate with Eve and communicated well, and Eve viewed the serpent as if it were somebody she could talk to and befriend. The serpent was no stranger. The "old serpent" mentioned in the third chapter from the end of the Bible (Revelation 20:2) clearly seems to refer to this serpent in the third chapter from the beginning of the Bible (Genesis 3) and identifies him as Satan, the Devil.

Being very crafty and intelligent, the serpent presumably would have spent considerable time getting acquainted with Eve. This, it would seem, was vital since any wrong move that would allow Eve to detect his plot would mean the end of his grand plan for the downfall of mankind.

We do not know how old Adam was when he and Eve were cast out of the garden, but we can make a rough but plausible guess. It appears Adam was 130 years old when he fathered Seth (Genesis 5:3). It also appears Seth was born a short time after his eldest brother Cain killed the other brother Abel (Genesis 4:25), both of whom were already adults at the time. And since Eve apparently conceived Cain immediately after they left the garden (Genesis 4:1), we can surmise that Adam left the garden when he was around the age of 100. If this assumption is correct, there would have been plenty of opportunities for the serpent to befriend Eve.

The very fact Eve was alone chitchatting with the serpent also suggests that Adam had through some time grown confident enough in Eve to leave her alone while he attended to other duties. My observation is this: When a couple first get married, they tend to hold hands and go places together. They confide in each other every minute detail of their thoughts, emotions, pleasures, likes, and dislikes. As time passes, their confidence grows, and there are times when they are comfortable being temporarily apart.

Of course, the serpent picked the best moment to conduct his chitchat with his prey, Eve. The best opportunity was when Adam was not around. This would not be a one-off conversation but a continuing dialogue on numerous occasions over the years. The serpent had time on his side as he tried to win over the confidence of the intelligent woman, bit by bit.

No one really knows where the garden was located, largely because the landscape of the earth during Adam's life was very different from the present earth. Noah's flood radically changed the geography of the earth. However, from the account in Genesis 2, it appears the garden covered a huge area, and Adam probably needed to travel over this vast area on foot. Inevitably, the two beautiful people were separated for short periods of time. This presented great opportunities for the serpent to plan and carry out his deceptive strategy.

Sure enough, the serpent finally executed his grand plan, and both Eve and Adam fell for it. There are volumes of literature and commentaries on this satanic deception, and I will leave it to interested readers to pursue the study of it further. Suffice it to say, though, that to this day, Satan continues his deceptive work, seeking to lead Christians to betray our Lord God. He steadfastly employs the familiar tactic of mixing truth with a little falsehood, and many fall for it. Satan delights in seeing our marital relationships end in divorce, and we can see the fruit of his work even in the changing legal definition of marriage in our day.

The Downfall

> *And the LORD God said unto the serpent, Because you have done this, you are cursed above all cattle, and above every beast of the field; upon your belly shall you go, and dust shall you eat all the days of your life: And I will put enmity between you and the woman, and between your seed and her seed; he shall bruise your head, and you shall bruise his heel. Unto the woman he said, I will greatly multiply your sorrow and your conception; in sorrow you shall bring forth children; and your desire shall be to your husband, and he shall rule over you. And unto Adam he said, Because you have listened unto the voice of your wife, and have eaten of the tree, of which I commanded you, saying, You shall not eat of it: cursed is the ground for your sake; in sorrow shall you eat of it all the days of your life; Thorns also and thistles shall it*

> *bring forth to you; and you shall eat the plants of the field; In the sweat of your face shall you eat bread, till you return unto the ground; for out of it were you taken: for dust you are, and unto dust shall you return.*
> *Genesis 3:14–19*

The moment the woman and the man ate of the forbidden tree in disobedience to God's command, they lost their intimate relationship with God and incurred his punishment. The enmity between the woman and the serpent and their respective seeds foreshadowed the sacrifice of God's only begotten Son Jesus on the cross and Jesus' ultimate victory over Satan. In Christianity, the sacrifice of Jesus Christ for redemption from sins is often termed *salvation*. Salvation through faith in Christ is necessary to bring us back into the fold of God's love.

The punishments pronounced against the woman and the man also prepared them for the hostile environment they would enter when they were cast out of the garden. The division of duties between Adam and Eve ensured their survival. This shows God did care for the couple despite their disobedience. God did not abandon them, and he has not abandoned us. God has a great plan and wants to restore humanity to that original, intimate relationship with him.

Although it was Eve who committed the sin first, God first approached Adam to question him about the rebellious act.

> *And they heard the voice of the LORD God walking in the garden in the cool of the day: and Adam and his wife hid themselves from the presence of the LORD God among the trees of the garden. And the LORD God called unto Adam, and said unto him, Where are you?*
> *Genesis 3:8–9*

Why did God go after Adam first to call him to account rather than Eve? After all, she was the first to eat the forbidden fruit and then gave some to her husband. The answer lies in Genesis 3:17, when God said to Adam, "Because you have listened unto the voice of your wife." This, of course, does not mean husbands should never listen to their wives, but it does mean God wants husbands to lead. The command not to eat the forbidden fruit was given to Adam (as the leader) in the garden. Adam therefore had the primary responsibility to lead on this.

The Garden of Love

To rebuild and enrich our intimate relationship with God, Paul calls us to imitate God's love.

> *Be therefore followers of God . . . walk in love, as Christ also has loved us, and has given himself for us an offering and a sacrifice to God for a sweet smelling fragrance. . . . Wives, submit yourselves unto your own husbands, as unto the Lord. For the husband is the head of the wife, even as Christ is*

> *the head of the church: and he is the savior of the body. Therefore as the church is subject unto Christ, so let the wives be to their own husbands in every thing. Husbands, love your wives, even as Christ also loved the church, and gave himself for it. . . . That he might present it [i.e., the church] to himself a glorious church, not having spot, or wrinkle, or any such thing; but that it should be holy and without blemish. So ought men to love their wives as their own bodies. He that loves his wife loves himself. For no man ever yet hated his own flesh; but nourishes and cherishes it, even as the Lord the church: For we are members of his body, of his flesh, and of his bones. For this cause shall a man leave his father and mother, and shall be joined unto his wife, and they two shall be one flesh. This is a great mystery: but I speak concerning Christ and the church. Nevertheless let every one of you in particular so love his wife even as himself; and the wife see that she respect her husband.*
> *Ephesians 5:1-2, 22-25, 27–33*

The first thing we will note in these passages is this sentence in Ephesians 5:31: "For this cause shall a man leave his father and mother, and shall be joined unto his wife, and they two shall be one flesh." This is a quotation of Genesis 2:24. To recap, the verse in Genesis 2 refers to the sexual union of the two lovers as a means of expressing their love. This love is expressed at the highest level; it is pure, intimate, whole, complete, and holy. Although they were naked, they did not see themselves that way. They were in the enclosed garden, and their nakedness was not exposed to the outside world. God was present and walked with them, and their love for God was intimate, complete, and pure. There was no distinction between the love between Adam and Eve, and that between God and the human couple. Becoming one flesh was not just the union of the flesh but also the union of the two spirits; and the spirit comes from God.

When questioned about divorce, Jesus cited God's original intention for marriage.

> *And he answered and said unto them, Have you not read, that he who made them at the beginning made them male and female, And said, For this cause shall a man leave father and mother, and shall cleave to his wife: and they two shall be one flesh? Therefore they are no more two, but one flesh. What therefore God has joined together, let not man put asunder.*
> *Matthew 19:4–6*

Sexual union (i.e., marriage) is for life. Beside the necessity to reproduce for the survival of humanity, sex is also necessary to form the bond between husband and wife. What kind of relationship exists between a couple if they never have sex? At best, we perhaps could say they are close friends. However, a pair of close friends is not the same as a husband and wife, even if the couple are legally married. The bond of sex is unique to the husband and wife and can never be replaced by any other bond that may exist between individuals. God created sex, and sex is holy. A husband and wife need sex to build the bond that should exist between them. And bond building takes a lifetime of effort.

In Ephesians 5, Paul brings us back to the very first love again and makes the connection between union of the bodies and the union of the spirits. He shows us the way to achieve this. The union of bodies *and* spirits is the original intention of God. It represents the holy love God wants us to live and enjoy. This holy love can be attained in two ways: via sexual union in marriage and through celibacy in the unmarried. The sexual union we see in the garden is an example of the first case; Paul himself is an example of the latter case.

The Great Mystery

A few years ago, I met an old friend. We graduated from the same college but had lost touch with each other since. She had a happy-go-lucky type of personality and was very much liked by others. However, she did not like the "nagging" from her mother, and the two had been at loggerheads on many occasions. It was only when she got married and had children of her own that she realized and appreciated her mother's love, her protective nature, and her wholehearted devotion to her daughter's upbringing. If not for her mother, my friend would not be what she is today. She even noticed that her love for her children was exactly the same as how her mother had loved her. She now fully understands and appreciates her mother's love and care. It took her own experience as a mother to understand her mother's love.

God loves us, and he wants us to experience and appreciate his love. From the beginning of creation, he established the wonderful plan the apostle Paul called the "great mystery" (Ephesians 5:32). Paul was explaining the relationship between husband and wife—the love in the garden—and yet he said he was referring to the love between Christ and his church. To understand what he meant, we need to revisit the creation accounts yet again.

> *And God said, Let us make man in our image, after our likeness: and let them have dominion over the fish of the sea, and over the fowl of the air, and over the cattle, and over all the earth, and over every creeping thing that creeps upon the earth. So God created man in his own image, in the image of God created he him; male and female created he them. And God blessed them, and God said unto them, Be fruitful, and multiply, and fill the earth, and subdue it: and have dominion over the fish of the sea, and over the fowl of the air, and over every living thing that moves upon the earth.*
> *Genesis 1:26-28*

Recall that Genesis 1 is about creation before the Garden of Eden was presented. God's plan is revealed in verse 26: the creation of man in God's *image* and his *likeness*. However, during the creation process depicted in verse 27, only God's image is mentioned. Since God's intention was to create man in his image and likeness, we would expect that both the image and likeness of God are incorporated in humans.

The word for "image" in Hebrew is *tselem* (*tseh'-lem*), which means shadow or shade, representation of substance, resemblance, phantom, or illusion. On the other hand, "likeness" in Hebrew is *demuth* (*dem-ooth'*). It means resemblance, model, shape, fashion, manner, or similitude. Thus, *image* refers to the shape or shadow of God, whereas *likeness* refers to the manner or characteristics of God.

There are numerous passages in the Bible where image (*tseh'-lem*) is mentioned and from which we can derive its meaning. We will look at just enough of these to deduce its significance.

> *Then you shall drive out all the inhabitants of the land from before you, and destroy all their engraved stones, and destroy all their molten images, and demolish all their high places.*
> *Numbers 33:52*

In the plains of Moab by the Jordan, God commanded Moses to destroy all the idols and the places where they were worshiped in Moab. These idols were made of wood and other materials and shaped into the images of beasts and heavenly bodies.

> *You have also taken your fair jewels of my gold and of my silver, which I had given you, and made to yourself images of men, and did commit harlotry with them, And took your embroidered garments,*

and covered them: and you have set my oil and my incense before them.
Ezekiel 16:17–18

Here Ezekiel was revealing what God had said to him about the sins of the Israelites. So the images mentioned in Numbers and Ezekiel refer to the castings and carvings of images, shapes, or forms of objects such as animals, humans, or heavenly bodies, representing their gods or deities. By the same reasoning, we could deduce that the *image of God* implies that God does have a form or shape so that God can cast an image of himself.

And the LORD appeared unto him [Abraham] by the oaks of Mamre: and he sat in the tent door in the heat of the day; And he lifted up his eyes and looked, and, lo, three men stood by him: and when he saw them, he ran to meet them from the tent door, and bowed himself toward the ground, And said, My Lord, if now I have found favor in your sight, pass not away, I pray you, from your servant: Let a little water, I pray you, be fetched, and wash your feet, and rest yourselves under the tree: And I will fetch a morsel of bread, and comfort your hearts; after that you shall pass on: for therefore are you come to your servant. And they said, So do, as you have said.
Genesis 18:1–5

Here we see that Abraham saw three *men,* and one of them was God. Abraham worshiped him, and the "man" did not reject this. In fact, Genesis 18:17

confirms that this one man was indeed the Lord (*yeh-ho-vaw'*). Abraham offered to wash his feet and to bring food for the three visitors to eat, and they ate (Genesis 18:8). In verses 9 and 10, we also see that God and the two who accompanied him (angels) spoke to Abraham.

> *And they [angels] said unto him, Where is Sarah your wife? And he said, Behold, in the tent. And he [God] said, I will certainly return unto you according to the time of life; and, lo, Sarah your wife shall have a son.*
> *Genesis 18:9–10*

Thus, it appears here that God does have a body and feet, and he could speak. To Abraham he looked like a man, and he could eat the food Abraham prepared. Jesus himself also indicates that God has a voice and a form.

> *And the Father himself, who has sent me, has borne witness of me. You have neither heard his voice at any time, nor seen his form.*
> *John 5:37*

However, this seems to contradict the traditional notion that God is a spirit and therefore is invisible, as the following verses suggest.

> *God is a Spirit: and they that worship him must worship him in spirit and in truth.*
> *John 4:24*

> *[Jesus] is the image of the invisible God, the firstborn of all creation.*
> *Colossians 1:15*

The traditional argument is that since God is invisible, he therefore has no shape, nor can he cast a shadow. This assumption is based on the reasoning that if something is invisible, it must be without form. Most scientists now believe that beside known matter, there is also unknown matter out there somewhere, such as dark matter. In other words, it is possible that there are things out there that are invisible and yet they still exist. The Bible tells us this, in fact, is so. In 2 Kings 6, the prophet Elisha and his servant Gehazi were surrounded by the great army of the king of Syria.

> *And when the servant of the man of God [i.e., Elisha is the man of God] was risen early, and gone forth, behold, an army compassed the city both with horses and chariots. And his servant said unto him, Alas, my master! what shall we do? And he answered, Fear not: for they that be with us are more than they that be with them. And Elisha prayed, and said, LORD, I pray you, open his eyes, that he may see. And the LORD opened the eyes of the young man; and he saw: and, behold, the mountain was full of horses and chariots of fire round about Elisha.*
> *2 Kings 6:15–17*

Of course, these horses and chariots of fire were the spiritual army of God. Originally they were invisible to the servant of Elisha. Elisha then prayed to God to give his servant the ability to see. Elisha did not pray that God's spiritual army would reveal themselves to his servant. He prayed that God would give his servant the special ability to see this army. What Elisha and his servant saw were the original, invisible shapes of God's spiritual army.

Paul experienced something similar when he was on his way to Damascus to persecute Christians. He was confronted by the resurrected Christ Jesus and was converted. Later he gave an account of his encounter to the apostles in Jerusalem.

> *And I fell unto the ground, and heard a voice saying unto me, Saul, Saul, why do you persecute me? And I answered, Who are you, Lord? And he said unto me, I am Jesus of Nazareth, whom you persecute. And they that were with me saw indeed the light, and were afraid; but they heard not the voice of him that spoke to me.*
> Acts 22:7–9

Those around Paul could see the light but could not hear the voice of Jesus. There are many more passages in the Scriptures that indicate God has form and body parts. He has a face (Numbers 12:8), hands (Psalm 111:7), fingers (Exodus 31:18), hair (Daniel 7:9), arms (Psalm 44:3), and lips (Isaiah 11:4), to name just a few. Indeed, if God has no form, how could Jesus sit at his right hand?

> *Who is he that condemns? It is Christ that died, yea rather, that is risen again, who is even at the right hand of God, who also makes intercession for us.*
> Romans 8:34

It does not matter whether *right hand* is a figure of speech. The expression connotes positioning. God must occupy a position in order to refer to Jesus being at a certain position in relation to him. That is, he must have a form. It is hard to be convinced that God does not have a form when the Bible is overwhelmed with scriptures that say he has. All those instances cannot be easily dismissed as merely metaphorical. Many scholars believe the shape, or form, in these cases is what is commonly termed a "theophany," a physical manifestation of God in such a form so that humans can see, although this does not explain cases like those experienced by Elisha and the apostle Paul.

From all this we can at least infer that God is not void or empty. He must have a form (as confirmed by Jesus in John 5:37), although it is hard to visualize what this form is. The form is invisible, but God can choose to manifest himself to us. Alternatively, God may enable our eyes to see his form, as Elisha and his servant did. Undeniably, the Lord is there (*yeh-ho-vaw' shawm*—Ezekiel 48:35).

Another aspect of God's form is raised by King Solomon's prayer upon the completion of the temple he built for the Lord God.

> *And now, O God of Israel, let your word, I pray you, be confirmed, which you spoke unto your servant David my father. But will God indeed dwell on the earth? Behold, the heaven and heaven of heavens cannot contain you; how much less this house that I have built? Yet have you respect unto the prayer of your servant, and to his supplication, O LORD my God, to hearken unto the cry and to the prayer, which your servant prays before you today: That your eyes may be open toward this house night and day, even toward the place of which you have said, My name shall be there: that you may hearken unto the prayer which your servant shall make toward this place.*
> 1 Kings 8:26–29

Solomon was well aware that even heaven and the heaven of heavens could not contain God, let alone this earthly temple. When Solomon said the temple could not contain his Lord God, we are inclined to conclude that God must be bigger than that huge temple. However, Solomon also said that his God was in heaven. Perhaps Solomon was comparing the Jerusalem temple with the glorious dwellings God inhabits in heaven. In that sense, Solomon's temple was but a shed! But it was the thought that counted!

Now, let me put forward an interesting question: Since God has a form, and therefore presumably can be bodily present only at one place at a time, how do we explain that God is present in so many gatherings all over the world—in communion services, Bible study groups, prayer meetings, and so on—all at the same time? On the one hand, Jesus has told us God the Father is in heaven (e.g., Matthew 6:9; Mark 11:26). On the other hand, the Bible confirms that God is omnipresent; that is, he is present everywhere all at the same time.

> *Am I a God at hand, says the LORD, and not a God afar off? Can any hide himself in secret places that I shall not see him? says the LORD. Do not I fill heaven and earth? says the LORD.*
> *Jeremiah 23:23–24*

King David also realized that he could not escape the presence of God.

> *If I ascend up into heaven, you are there: if I make my bed in Sheol, behold, you are there.*
> *Psalm 139:8*

This is a question we simply cannot answer with certainty. Indeed, there are still many aspects of God we do not understand or have the ability to comprehend because we are physically trapped in time and three-dimensional space. Perhaps, as many Christians believe, God is huge and covers the whole universe. Or perhaps he has a certain size but his power and might certainly extend over the whole universe and beyond, much like the ruler of a country, who may reside in a certain state but is still able to administer the whole country. Similarly, God can govern the whole universe from heaven. He has a whole army of able angels and perhaps some other forms that are not revealed in the Bible to govern for him.

Being created in God's image means that in a certain sense we are the projection of his form, although we may not know exactly what the resemblances are because the Fall has had an impact on our body. What we do know is that even though this body of ours is corruptible, it is still far superior to that of all the creatures on earth. Adam and Eve needed their superior bodies to survive and multiply. We need our bodies to manage and control creation. No matter how imperfect (due to the Fall), our bodies still retain the image of God and thus some resemblance to him.

Because we are created in his image, God cares about our body more than we do. That is why when we abuse or misuse our body, God is furious. Paul describes the wickedness of those who abuse their bodies.

> *Therefore God also gave them up to uncleanness through the lusts of their own hearts, to dishonor their own bodies between themselves: Who changed the truth of God into a lie, and worshiped and served the creature more than the Creator, who is blessed forever. Amen. For this cause God gave them up unto vile affections: for even their women did change the natural use into that which is against nature: And likewise also the men, leaving the natural use of the woman, burned in their lust one toward another; men with men working that which is shameful, and receiving in themselves that recompense of their error which was fitting. And even as they did not like to retain God in their*

knowledge, God gave them over to a reprobate mind, to do those things which are not proper; Being filled with all unrighteousness, fornication, wickedness, covetousness, maliciousness; full of envy, murder, debate, deceit, malignity; whisperers, Backbiters, haters of God, despiteful, proud, boasters, inventors of evil things, disobedient to parents, Without understanding, covenant breakers, without natural affection, implacable, unmerciful: Who knowing the judgment of God, that they who commit such things are worthy of death, not only do the same, but have pleasure in them that do them. Romans 1:24–32

In the eyes of God, our body is holy because our body is created in his image. In fact, Jesus himself bears the image of the invisible God, and when he came into this world, he took on the form of physical human flesh.

[Jesus] is the image of the invisible God, the firstborn of all creation.
Colossians 1:15

And the Word [Jesus] was made flesh, and dwelt among us full of grace and truth.
John 1:14

Christians are children of God and enjoy an inheritance from him. However, image is merely a shadow of the object. Other than the differences in appearance, the image of God does not provide much distinction from, say, an animal, in terms of its functionalities. If we were created *only* with God's image, we would be more intelligent than those other creatures, but we would still lack the "God" qualities that make us what we are and distinguish us from animals.

This brings us to the second point: the *likeness (dem-ooth')* of God. The qualities unique to humans are the result of the likeness of God in them, qualities such as love, concern for others, mercy, purity of heart, truth seeking, honesty, righteousness, happiness, and appreciation of others.

God said two things about the creation of Adam and Eve.

> *Let us make man in our image, after our likeness.*
> *Genesis 1:26*

God then used earth to mold Adam according to his own image. He then blew into Adam's nostrils with his breath of life, and Adam became a living being. Most Christians agree that the breath of life refers to Adam's God-given spirit.

> *And the LORD God formed man of the dust of the ground, and breathed into his nostrils the breath of life; and man became a living soul.*
> *Genesis 2:7*

Thus Adam had his spirit as a gift from God, thus setting him apart from all creatures on earth. This gift enabled Adam and Eve to talk and walk with God.

This spirit is the equivalent of the likeness God mentioned in Genesis 1:26. However, after the Fall, this spiritual likeness and the image of God were damaged. In Genesis 5, the Bible describes the deterioration.

> *This is the book of the generations of Adam. In the day that God created man, in the likeness of God made He him; Male and female created He them; and blessed them, and called their name Adam, in the day when they were created. And Adam lived a hundred and thirty years, and begat a son in his own likeness, after his image; and called his name Seth.*
> *Genesis 5:1–3*

God created Adam in the likeness of God. However, when Adam fathered a son, Seth, that son was more like Adam himself than like God. This is the first sign of the deterioration of the likeness of God. Image is our outward appearance and shape, whereas likeness is our internal spiritual nature and characteristics. We often hear the phrase "like father like son" or "like mother like daughter." These expressions do not refer to the external image of parent and child but to the similarity of their characteristics: their nature, posture, behavior, thinking, and so on. These can be acquired only over time. The likeness of God in man has been damaged by the Fall, but that likeness remains. As we walk closer and closer to God, that likeness grows. This is what Christians often refer to as spiritual growth and maturity. Hence, Paul urges Christians to be filled with knowledge, wisdom, and understanding of God, and to walk the way of Jesus. Walking is a learning process, and it takes time to learn. We take a step at a time when we walk.

> *For this cause we also, since the day we heard it, do not cease to pray for you, and to desire that you might be filled with the knowledge of his will in all wisdom and spiritual understanding; That you might walk worthy of the Lord, fully pleasing, being fruitful in every good work, and increasing in the knowledge of God; Strengthened with all might, according to his glorious power, unto all patience and longsuffering with joyfulness; Giving thanks unto the Father, who has made us fit to be partakers of the inheritance of the saints in light: Who has delivered us from the power of darkness, and has translated us into the kingdom of his dear Son: In whom we have redemption through his blood, even the forgiveness of sins.*
> *Colossians 1:9–14*

So, with this insight into the creation of man in the image and likeness of God, let us return to that great mystery of God's love for the church and how it relates to the husband-and-wife relationship. We possess the likeness of God, yet we are to grow more and more like God daily. As we grow more like him in love, his love will fill our marriages. Paul highlights a few very significant steps we can take in order to experience this divine plan of holy love: Be followers of God, walk in love, and redeem the time.

Be followers of God.

> *Be you therefore followers of God, as dear children.*
> Ephesians 5:1

This is another way of saying God is our master, and we are his apprentices, or disciples. To become an apprentice of God, of course, we need to confess and repent of our sins and receive Jesus as our personal Savior. This is a prerequisite. The effect is that our spiritual relationship with God, which was once severed because of the fall of Adam and Eve, is reestablished. In Ephesians 5:2 and Romans 3:23–28, Paul tells us that we are saved from (spiritual) death because Jesus died in our place. By accepting Jesus and believing in him, Paul says we are led by the Holy Spirit of God and are sons (and daughters) of God (Romans 8:14). By being cleansed by the blood of Jesus (his death), we are born again into a new spiritual being. This does not mean Christians will never commit sinful acts. We still dwell in this physical body and are constantly tempted by Satan and seduced by worldly matters. But to be a follower of God means we are prepared to be trained by God. We desire to imitate God in the way he loves us.

The other day I read an article in a local community newspaper about couples looking more like each other as they get older. One theory for why this seems to be the case is that the couple tend to imitate each other or are influenced by each other's behavior, thinking, and habits. I think there is some truth to this. I have met a few old couples myself who have such similar outlooks, behaviors, and habits, one might almost think they were twins.

Paul wants us to imitate God, not his power but his love. God loves every being. He loves the poor. He loves the rich. At the same time he is righteous, and his laws never change. His love does not overlook sin, but his love for us is so intense that he was willing to sacrifice his treasured Son for us. The more we imitate God, the more we are like God. But we are not trying to be like God in the sense that Satan was—by trying to be as powerful as God. Rather, we want to be like God in his love and holiness.

Walk in love. That is, we are to walk in *God's* love.

> *And walk in love, as Christ also has loved us, and has given himself for us an offering and a sacrifice to God.*
> *Ephesians 5:2*

The word *as* (*kath-oce'*) means "according to" or "inasmuch as." This implies that we are to walk in love in response to the love exemplified by Jesus. Jesus set the example by showing his love to his church, and Paul has shown us how Christians should respond to his love.

Walking in love means loving God and loving your spouse. Walking implies a series of steps, a constant forward movement in the same direction, in harmony and in resonance. It is alive. Dead men do not walk. Walking in love rules out fornication (Ephesians 5:3) and other sinful actions and speech (vv. 4–5). But instead of enforcing these prohibitions as laws or rules, like the Ten Commandments, they are "engraved" on our hearts; thus there is nothing to remember and nothing to follow as an outward rule. They are in our hearts. We want to live the life of love, which is from God.

Jesus, as the head of the church, sacrificed his own life for the church. He is the source of love. So the husband, as the head of his wife, should make sacrifices for his wife. This is the way the husband shows his love at the highest level. As the church submits to Jesus, so does the wife submit herself to her husband (Ephesians 5:22–25). Here, Paul uses the head and body functionality and relationship to illustrate the proper order and the different roles in marriage set down by God. Some readers may have issues with this order and find Paul's command of submission hard to swallow. I urge you to read on. There are reasons for this order, and once this is understood, the order can be better appreciated. To walk in love entails a dynamic, two-way, bond-building process. Christ loves his church, just as the husband is to love his wife. His church responds by submitting to him, just as the wife is to submit herself to her husband. Through their mutual love, both husband and wife will have a better understanding of the love between Christ and his church.

Redeem the time.

> *Have no fellowship with the unfruitful works of darkness, but rather reprove them. For it is a shame even to speak of those*

> *things which are done of them in secret. But all things that are reproved are made manifest by the light: for whatsoever does make manifest is light. Therefore he says, Awake you that sleep, and arise from the dead, and Christ shall give you light. See then that you walk carefully, not as fools, but as wise, Redeeming the time, because the days are evil. Therefore be not unwise, but understanding what the will of the Lord is. And be not drunk with wine, in which is excess; but be filled with the Spirit; Speaking to yourselves in psalms and hymns and spiritual songs, singing and making melody in your heart to the Lord; Giving thanks always for all things unto God, even the Father, in the name of our Lord Jesus Christ.*
> *Ephesians 5:11–20*

Ephesians 5 is about love. Hence, we need to read the above verses in the context of love. The word translated "redeem" has two connotations. *Adam Clarke's Commentary* describes it as "buying up those moments (times) which others seem to throw away."[18] In other words, do not waste time on things like drunkenness, engaging in activities that belong to the dark side (i.e., Satan), lusts, adulteries, and so on. In his commentary, John Gill denotes it as "a careful and diligent use of it (time), an improvement of it to the best advantage; and shows that it is valuable and precious."[19] In other words, we are to diligently save up time and build the love bonds—the bond between the couple and God; the bond between husband and wife—and introduce God's love to our neighbors. We are to manage our time wisely.

In the Ten Commandments, God purposefully set aside one day of the week as a "rest day." All Israelites were to observe this day, called the Sabbath, as a holy day. According to Israel's traditions, this day starts at nightfall on Friday and ends on Saturday evening. It is the seventh day of the week. Most churches keep Sunday as the holy day and as a day in remembrance of Christ's resurrection. It is appropriate that we keep one day of the week as the day we can rest and do holy things—a day husband and wife can love God together and think about good things they can do together, a day husband and wife can get to know and love each other better, a day we can show our kindness to our neighbors, a day we can redeem solely for love, a day we can learn more about love, and a day we can express the kind of love that is characterized by God himself (1 John 4:8).

To build an intimate bond with God, we must learn to imitate Jesus' love for his church, and that begins by submitting to him. Jesus' love for us was exhibited by sacrificing his life for us. In response, we are to love him by submitting to him, and then we are to love others with sacrificial love. Such sacrificial love is especially necessary in marriage.

With the Fall, our bond with God was broken, and we felt the emptiness in ourselves. We wanted to belong to God, but we were unable to reestablish the bond. That is why Jesus came into this world and revealed himself to us. His death and resurrection has provided salvation for us and paved the way for us to rebuild this bond with God. For most Christians, this bond is very weak because we are very weak spiritually. Unless we willingly accept God's love, the bond will remain weak and may eventually break. Jesus illustrates this via a parable.

> *Behold, a sower went forth to sow; And when he sowed, some seeds fell by the wayside, and the fowls came and devoured them up: Some fell upon stony places, where they had not much earth: and immediately they sprung up, because they had no deepness of earth: And when the sun was up, they were scorched; and because they had no root, they withered away. And some fell among thorns; and the thorns sprung up, and choked them: But others fell into good ground, and brought forth fruit, some a hundredfold, some sixtyfold, some thirtyfold.*
> *Matthew 13:3–8*

Jesus forewarns us that if we do not persevere in building our bond with God, soon we will find we are being robbed of this bond by the world's temptations. We have to open up to God, seek his wisdom, let the Holy Spirit fill our heart, and talk and walk with God. Only then will our intimate relationship with God strengthen.

Our bond with God is established by God's Holy Spirit residing in us, and that bond is strengthened as we walk with God. The bond between husband and wife is established by their sexual relationship, and it grows strong as they imitate the love between Jesus and his church. It is through the love between husband and wife that we come to understand and fully appreciate the love between Jesus and his church. Of course, there are Christians, like Paul, who are strong in faith and spirit, and their bond with Jesus is strong; yet they prefer to remain unmarried and celibate. For the majority of us, though, one way to imitate God's love and to walk in God's love is through the roles of husband and wife.

Bond Building

Paul concedes that the love bond between husband and wife is a great mystery; and so is the love bond between Jesus and Christians. Even in this modern era, we still do not fully understand the what's and how's of the bond between a couple. An onlooker probably will never comprehend how strong the bond is. Only the husband and wife themselves can feel, taste, appreciate, and long for it. It is invisible but real. So is the bond between God and Christians. It is invisible but real, and it takes time to appreciate the intimate relationship. The bond grows as one matures spiritually. Some mature faster than others, and some, like the apostle Paul, attain spiritual maturity apart from marriage, opting for celibacy. For the majority of us, however, God has provided us an alternative pathway to improve our relationship with him. This is what Paul is getting at in Ephesians 5.

In essence, Paul is saying that the relationship between Jesus and the church is similar to that between a husband and wife. We can strengthen our relationship with God by learning from the roles of husband and wife in their marriage. We can also improve the intimate relationship between husband and wife by learning from the relationship between Jesus and the church.

HEAD AND BODY

God is preparing us to one day be united with Jesus as his bride.

> *Come here, I [the angel] will show you [apostle John] the bride, the Lamb's wife.*
> *Revelation 21:9*

The Bible does not elaborate further on this relationship. Most scholars concur that the Lamb's wife is a symbol of a future spiritual relationship between Christ Jesus and his church. We know that there will be no marriage or sexual differences among those in heaven, and we will be like angels, that is, spiritual.

> *Jesus answered and said unto them [the Sadducees], You do err, not knowing the scriptures, nor the power of God. For in the resurrection they [the dead] neither marry, nor are given in marriage, but are as the angels of God in heaven.*
> *Matthew 22:29–30*

We also know that there is no difference between the races, whether Jews or Greek or others, for we are all spiritual in Christ Jesus.

> *There is neither Jew nor Greek, there is neither bond nor free, there is neither male nor female: for you are all one in Christ Jesus.*
> *Galatians 3:28*

Thus, in heaven we will enjoy a very special relationship with Jesus, although we do not have many details about it.

> *For your Maker is your husband; the LORD of hosts is his name; and your Redeemer the Holy One of Israel; The God of the whole earth shall he be called.*
> *Isaiah 54:5*

Thus, idolatry is prohibited by the second commandment because it constitutes committing spiritual adultery, or unfaithfulness against Jesus, the spiritual Husband.[20] God designed the intimate relationship between husband and wife to reveal a glimpse of this future relationship. Yet even Paul admits that the love between Christ and the church, as well as between husband and wife, is a great mystery.

> *For this cause shall a man leave his father and mother, and shall be joined unto his wife, and they two shall be one flesh. This is a great mystery: but I speak concerning Christ and the church.*

Secrets of First Love
Ephesians 5:31–32

The love between Christ and the church is all-inclusive between them but also exclusive in that it is limited to Christ and the church. They are essentially one flesh, with Christ as the head and the church as the body. Between them exists a unique bond and intimate understanding of one another. We gain a glimpse of this great mystery of divine love through the manifestation of the love between a husband and his wife. In this intimate relationship, God wants the husband to play the leading role.

For the husband is the head of the wife, even as Christ is the head of the church.
Ephesians 5:23

It is a misconception that the husband is the "head of the household." Certainly the husband has a say in the house. However, he does not have the full authority over it. The home is managed by both spouses, to the best of their abilities and for the betterment of the family. Hence, both husband and wife are equally responsible for its well-being. Nowhere in the Bible does it indicate that the husband is the head of the household.

Ephesians 5:23 does not say the husband *should be* the head. It says the husband *is* the head. It is by divine design that the husband is the head. Like the birth order of siblings, it is a fact that cannot be altered. It is a matter of proper order and does not suggest the husband is in any way superior to his wife. In fact, he may possess fewer skills and abilities than his wife.

We often confuse biblical headship, or leadership, with common ideas of what a leader is or should be. A leader is commonly believed to be one who possesses certain traits such as power, vision and values, compassion, integrity, charisma, and intelligence. It is generally accepted that with these traits a person is able to control or influence others to achieve common goals.[21] However, the biblical definition of a leader is quite different. Contrary to contemporary thinking, to be a leader in the biblical sense means to serve others, and this requires no particular skill or personality trait. It requires only a willingness to put others first.

> *Even as the Son of man came not to be ministered unto, but to minister, and to give his life a ransom for many.*
> *Matthew 20:28*

Jesus set down many leadership examples the husband can follow. John 13 describes Jesus washing the feet of his disciples on the night before the crucifixion. After performing the act, Jesus said this:

> *You call me Teacher and Lord: and you say rightly; for so I am. If I then, your Lord and Teacher, have washed your feet; you also ought to wash one another's feet. For I have given you an example, that you should do as I have done to you. Verily, verily, I say unto you, The servant is not greater than his lord; neither he that is sent greater than he*

> *that sent him. If you know these things, happy are you if you do them.*
> *John 13:13–17*

In a nutshell, Jesus was saying that one who takes the leadership role must be humble and prepared to do the lowliest act that shows love of others. In the context of the marital relationship, the husband is assigned the leadership role and is to do whatever it takes to show love for his wife, including the most humble acts.

Actually, *leader* is not a synonym for *head*. *Leader* implies that the one leading is a separate entity from those he or she leads. For example, a president or prime minister is the leader of a country of many citizens. These citizens may represent a variety of people, ethnicities, or associations who may act and make decisions independent of the leader. The leader and the citizens may have different and even conflicting interests. The head and the body do not function independently, however. Such a relationship calls for a different approach to leadership.

> *The Son of Man did not come to be served, but to serve, and to give His life a ransom for many.*
> *Matthew 20:28 (NKJV)*

The apostle Paul urges husbands to follow the example set by Jesus and love their wives by making sacrifices for them.

> *Husbands, love your wives, even as Christ also loved the church, and gave himself for it.*
> *Ephesians 5:25*

Paul does not say that husbands are to love their wives as Jesus loved the church. He says husbands are to love their wives and make sacrifices for them, as Jesus did for his church. Paul wants husbands to imitate and manifest the love of Jesus to their wives by making sacrifices for their benefit. To lead is to serve. To love is to sacrifice.

Head and body imply a cohesive oneness, or being. Hence, we have the biblical phrase, "the two become one flesh," implying that husband and wife are one "person," or being. It is not about who is superior or subordinate. We see this emphasis in Paul's description of the church as a body.

> *And the eye cannot say unto the hand, I have no need of you: nor again the head to the feet, I have no need of you. Nay, much more those members of the body, which seem to be more feeble, are necessary: And those members of the body, which we think to be less honorable, upon these we bestow more abundant honor; and our less respectable parts have greater respect. For our more respectable parts have no need: but God has arranged the body together, having given more abundant honor to that part which lacked: That there should be no schism in the body; but that the members should have the same care one for another. And whether one member suffers, all the members suffer with it; or one member be honored,*

> *all the members rejoice with it. Now you are the body of Christ, and members in particular.*
> 1 Corinthians 12:21–27

A horse, for example, has no problem at all coordinating actions between its head and body parts. The head and body always live in harmony, and their actions are always in agreement. That is the kind of marital life God wants husband and wife to live. By divine designation, God assigns the husband to be the head and the wife to be the body. This is more than just leadership, and it is not a master-and-slave relationship. God wants the husband to take full responsibility for the body, the whole marital being.

Problems emerge when the head and body each want to go its own way. In modern society, the norm is for both the body and the head to claim to be leaders and "equal partners." As such, the distinction between what is confined to the bedroom and what is outside becomes blurred and indistinguishable and often totally nonexistent. Every decision requires consensus. Even sex becomes a mutual bargain, rather than a matter of taking care of the needs of the other. Instead of fighting for survival of the family, each partner pursues his or her own personal interests and ambitions. We need to go back to the original, divine designation of roles. The husband needs to be not only the leader but also the head. In fact, he *is* the head by divine order.

Jesus set an excellent example as the head of the church. It is by being the imitator of Jesus that the husband learns and attains the quality of being a leader and head of the body.

Being part of the marital being, it is natural for the head to make sacrifices for the needs of the body, as Paul explained in Ephesians 5:28-29.

> *So ought men to love their wives as their own bodies. He that loves his wife loves himself. For no man ever yet hated his own flesh; but nourishes and cherishes it.*
> *Ephesians 5:28-29*

The husband treats his wife as if she is part of his flesh. When she is sick, he feels sick; when she is in pain, he feels pain too; when she is happy; he rejoices too. His "body" (i.e., his wife) is under his care, and he is obliged to nourish and cherish it.

SACRIFICIAL LOVE

> *Husbands, love your wives, even as Christ also loved the church, and gave himself for it.*
> *Ephesians 5:25*

The command to husbands to love their wives is much more than mere rhetoric. In the Christian community, it is generally accepted that husbands must make sacrifices. However, exactly what these sacrifices are remains a mystery to many. Some suggest it means the husband should be the breadwinner and take care of the needs of the family. Some even include tending the garden, taking care of children, taking up a second job, and helping out with the daily chores at home as sacrifices. Are these really sacrifices?

> *And unto Adam he [God] said, Because you have listened unto the voice of your wife, and have eaten of the tree, of which I commanded you, saying, You shall not eat of it: cursed is the ground for your sake; in sorrow shall you eat of it all the days of your life; Thorns also and thistles shall it bring forth to you; and you shall eat the plants of the field; In the sweat of your face shall you eat bread, till you return unto the ground; for out of it were you taken: for dust you are, and unto dust shall you return.*
> Genesis 3:17–19

Adam was punished for disobedience to God's command not to eat the forbidden fruit. He was to till the ground and work very hard in order to feed himself and his family. So, the extensive labor required to provide food, clothing, shelter, and protection is part of the punishment. It is not a sacrifice but a normal part of life and survival of the family unit in this world.

Some suggest the husband's sacrifice is the willingness to sacrifice his life for his wife. It is true, of course, that husbands should be prepared even to sacrifice their lives for their wives. However, what are the chances such sacrifice actually will ever be necessary? Almost nil. Jesus was born into this world with the ultimate purpose of sacrificing his life for us. We are not. Furthermore, as Christians our lives belong to Jesus, for he redeems us with his blood and life.

Christ has redeemed us from the curse of the law.
Galatians 3:13

For you are bought with a price: therefore glorify God in your body, and in your spirit, which are God's.
1 Corinthians 6:20

Our life belongs to Jesus. It does not belong to us or to our spouse. Therefore, we cannot claim to sacrifice a life that no longer belongs to us.

Another popular proposition is that husbands sacrifice by giving up their most treasured entertainments, such as watching football or playing golf, in order to spend more time with their wives. That is a laudable act. However, each individual has his own treasured entertainments, and they differ from person to person. Some may not even have one. Giving up our beloved pastime is a very small price to pay compared to what Jesus has given up. Besides this, wives can and often have made such sacrifices too. This is not unique to husbands only. Paul specifies that husbands, not wives, are to make sacrifices. There must be something else common among husbands that they are called to surrender. We will learn in chapter 6 that this is the sacrifice of their own sexual pleasure in order to achieve the sexual fulfillment of their wives.

Anyway, we just got away from a to-do list and into a giving-up list, didn't we? We like lists because they give us the false sense that we are in control. Adhering to and acting on the basis of a list is a challenge we often embrace. However, there is a good chance something ought to be on the list but is not. God gave us a list too: the Ten Commandments. And our efforts to keep them fail miserably. That is why Jesus gave us a shorter version of the commandments and put them in our hearts.

> *This is the covenant that I will make with them after those days, says the Lord, I will put my laws into their hearts, and in their minds will I write them.*
> *Hebrews 10:16*

The laws Jesus refers to, of course, are his commandments of love—to love God and to love our neighbor. Love is to characterize all our interactions in life. And it is Christ-like love especially that is to govern our marriages.

SUBMISSIVE LOVE

The wife is the flesh and bones of her husband (Genesis 2:23), as the church is the flesh and bones of Jesus (Ephesians 5:30). Paul went on to quote Genesis 2:24 and connected this to the bond between Jesus and his church (Ephesians 5:31–32). Just as the church is one body, so the sexual union of husband and wife makes them one flesh. And just as the Head (Christ) and the body (Christians) have different roles in the church, so husbands and wives have different roles in the one-flesh relationship we call marriage. So, how should the wife behave or function in relation to her husband?

> *Wives, submit yourselves unto your own husbands, as unto the Lord.*
> *Ephesians 5:22*

This verse has given rise to much controversy and many interpretations. Many questions and arguments have been put forward. Here are some examples.

I accept that a wife should submit to her husband. But why should my husband be the one who makes all the decisions, and why should he have everything his way?

What if my husband is abusive? Do I have to follow his directives and demands?

If submissiveness means full compliance without regarding consent and agreement, I find that hard to swallow.

To me, submissiveness means male oppression of females. This does not seem right, for we read of many instances in the Bible where females are protected and their status in society lifted and not suppressed.

My husband provides financially all the needs of my family, but when it comes to everything else—meals, outings, children's schooling, sports, even the home we live in—I'm the one in charge. I can't imagine I have to let him make all these decisions.

If I submit myself to my husband, will I become a doormat for him to walk on?

Again, we note that many of these so-called issues or concerns involve day-to-day housekeeping duties and are therefore nonissues. We dealt with this earlier. In chapter 2, we also read the oracle of King Lemuel in Proverbs 31, where the woman is praised and honored and her status in society upheld. All these activities have nothing to do with submissiveness. Submission as commanded by Paul is about the marriage bond.

The apostle Peter also talks about submission in his first epistle. However, he was speaking in a different context. His letter was addressed to the Christians (especially Christian Jews) in exile throughout the provinces of Asia Minor (1 Peter 1:1), who were suffering under trials and persecution. Peter urged these Christians living in such a hostile environment as aliens and exiles to be vigilant and honest in their conduct so that by their good deeds they could win over some enemies (1 Peter 2:12). He also urged them to submit themselves to the ruling authorities.

> *Submit yourselves to every ordinance of man for the Lord's sake: whether it be to the king, as supreme; Or unto governors, as unto them that are sent by him for the punishment of evildoers, and for the praise of them that do well. For so is the will of God, that with well doing you may put to silence the ignorance of foolish men: As free, and not using*

> *your liberty for a cloak of maliciousness, but as the servants of God. Honor all men. Love the brotherhood. Fear God. Honor the king. Servants, be subject to your masters with all fear; not only to the good and gentle, but also to the harsh.*
> *1 Peter 2:13–18*

Peter was talking about submission to the laws and official practices of the land while in exile as a means to win over the friendship of the land. This submissiveness had a specific and desirable purpose under such hostile circumstances. Paul's teaching was in a totally different context. Both Peter and Paul use the same word for submissiveness (*hupotasso*). However, the background and contexts of the passages show that Peter and Paul mean different things and have different purposes for submission. Therefore, to quote what Paul says in Ephesians 5 to either interpret or explain away what Peter says in his first epistle, or vice versa, is inappropriate.

Peter goes on to explain how husbands and wives should behave in the hostile environment his readers were facing.

> *Likewise, you wives, be in subjection to your own husbands; that, if any obey not the word, they also may without the word be won by the conduct of the wives.*
> *1 Peter 3:1*

Peter begins with "likewise" or "similarly." The purpose of the instruction does not change; it is still to win over someone who is hostile. The word translated "subjection" here is the same word translated "submit" in 1 Peter 2:13. In this case, the wives were Christians and their husbands were not. Although both Peter and Paul use the same word for "submit" (*hoop-ot-as'-so*) when commanding wives to submit to their husbands, they do not have the same semantics and application or serve the same purpose. Peter clearly intends submission as a means to calm down hostility, win over friendship, and ultimately convert unbelieving husbands to Christ.

> *While they behold your chaste behavior coupled with fear. Whose adorning let it not be that outward adorning of braiding the hair, and of wearing of gold, or of putting on of apparel; But let it be the hidden man of the heart, in that which is not corruptible, even the ornament of a meek and quiet spirit, which is in the sight of God of great price. For after this manner in former times the holy women also, who trusted in God, adorned themselves, being in subjection unto their own husbands: Even as Sara obeyed Abraham, calling him lord: whose daughters you are, as long as you do well, and are not afraid with any terror.*
> 1 Peter 3:2–6

Peter wanted the believing wives in the hostile land to stay on moral high ground, adorn themselves appropriately as daughters of God, and serve their unbelieving husbands in an appropriate manner. In so doing, he cited as an example Sarah obeying her husband Abraham. It is important to note that

Abraham and Sarah also were living in an alien land. The word for "obeyed" (*hoop-ak-oo'-o*) in 1 Peter 3:6 is not the word used for "subjection," or submissiveness (*hoop-ot-as'-so*), in verse 1. This obedience is like that expected of children in relation to their parents. It implies a certain amount of outward appearances. Obedience is to be seen. Hence, we have the phrase "calling him lord." We need to grasp the gist of Peter's message. In a hostile environment, a believing wife needs to perform better than the unbelieving wives of the land. Submission in this context is definitely different from what Paul is commanding in Ephesians. This submission is performed outside the bedroom and is to be seen by people of the land.

When addressing the husbands, again Peter began with "likewise" and thus was referring to the hostile environment they were in and the purpose of submissiveness. Peter urged the husband to honor the wife and to protect her against the hostile environment.

> *Likewise, you husbands, dwell with them according to knowledge, giving honor unto the wife, as unto the weaker vessel, and as being heirs together of the grace of life; that your prayers be not hindered.*
> *1 Peter 3:7*

In view of the circumstances of the hostile land, Peter reemphasized the need to obey the laws and authority of the land and to live within its confinements. Peter restated the obvious, cautioning believers in exile to obey the strange laws and customs of the land.

By now, the reader would have been convinced that this is about survival. Peter is saying that Christians living in a hostile environment need to be seen as good citizens, good spouses, and good neighbors in the local community. This outward goodness begins at home, between husbands and wives. He wants the wives to be seen as submissive (obedient) to the husbands and husbands to be seen as protective and caring of the wives. He goes on to demand that Christians' lives exhibit Christ-like qualities, even if they suffer for doing so.

> *Finally, be all of one mind, having compassion one with another, love as brethren, be tender hearted, be courteous: Not rendering evil for evil, or railing for railing: but on the contrary blessing; knowing that you are unto this called, that you should inherit a blessing. For he that will love life, and see good days, let him refrain his tongue from evil, and his lips that they speak no guile: Let him turn away from evil, and do good; let him seek peace, and pursue it. For the eyes of the Lord are over the righteous, and his ears are open unto their prayers: but the face of the Lord is against them that do evil. And who is he that will harm you, if you be followers of that which is good? But if you suffer for righteousness' sake, happy are you: and, Be not afraid of their terror, neither be troubled;*
> 1 Peter 3:8–14

In other words, husbands and wives are to show the good qualities of Jesus Christ and at the same time conform to the expectations in the hostile land without engaging in the evil practices of the land. Peter's submissiveness is about upholding the family unit and surviving in a hostile environment without compromising the godly qualities the Lord expects of believers.

When I first came to Australia, it took me quite a while to adapt to the multicultural settings and the "alien" ways. I remember when the side door of my house was broken, I called a carpenter to repair it. Joyfully, he came and fixed it, but he left an open square at the top for the glass. I asked, "Are you coming back to finish the top?" "Oh no," he replied, "you have to call the glass vendor." Realizing that I was an alien, he added, "And also a painter."

My neighbors always seemed to be peeking at me, but they shied away from engaging in conversations. The Chinese restaurant down the road had just changed hands. The new owners also were from a foreign country and were struggling with the "English." Within a few weeks, the restaurant was hit with petrol bombs. I remember being in another restaurant and being unable to understand the "English" of a waitress, although she was a local and spoke fluent Australian English. Such are the "hostile" environments for aliens.

I am not saying all Australians are racists or are unkind toward strangers. When my car broke down on a country road, someone stopped by and helped me fix the tire. When I was at a park trying to do my barbecue, a motorcyclist stopped by and showed me how to do it. What I want to demonstrate is that it is up to Christians, as aliens, to be seen as good citizens, good friends, and good neighbors. The apostle Peter was spot on in requiring husbands and wives to show compassion and love to one another. Husbands are to be protective of the wives, and wives are to show obedience to their husbands while in a hostile land. Probably that was the custom and the expected norm of the land.

Today Christians are aliens in this world too, whether we like it or not. Sadly, many Christians practice exactly what the non-Christians around us practice and think exactly the way most non-Christians think. In fact, sometimes I really wonder whether we have forgotten why we are here. Aren't we supposed to show the way—the proper way, the right way—to our friends and neighbors? Jesus wants Christians to be light and salt to the world. Peter did not suggest that we be "one of them," forgetting our roots in Jesus.

In America, many schools have removed any symbols that may suggest Christianity. Some hotels have removed the Bibles from their rooms. We may live in peace, but the environment has an undercurrent of hostility. The other day, a colleague left behind two Christian books on the round discussion table near my desk. Another colleague came along, fuming. He threw them into the main garbage bin. To him, even leaving behind some books constitutes religious propaganda and should not be tolerated. We are in a different kind of hostile land. We need to heed Peter's advice. Peter's submissiveness is about survival and showing the world who we are. We live in this world and are to obey the laws of the land, but we are not part of this world. We are to live heavenly lives and never forget the purpose of our being called to Christ.

Submission is more than just obedience. That is, it is easier to obey than to submit. To obey, I simply execute the command given. I do not even have to have a positive attitude toward the command in order to obey it. I do not have to understand the purpose or the implications of obeying the command.

The submission Paul spoke of, on the other hand, is about the intimate, head-and-body relationship between husband and wife. It is about bond building and strengthening the relationship and improving the communication between them. The head and body are inseparable and interdependent. The body responds to the head, supplementing and complementing its lead and fulfilling its goal and purpose.

The Greek word for submit *(hoop-ot-as'-so)* means to subordinate oneself, to obey, to be in subjection to, to submit oneself unto. It is also used in a military sense of arranging troops under the command of a military leader. Thus, the word implies having a voluntary attitude of yielding, cooperating, and assuming responsibility to accomplish the goal of a leader. It is not just about obeying. It is about proactively engaging and carrying out the mission. This requires a certain amount of understanding of, trust in, and respect for the officer in charge.

Submission to the husband requires the wife to willingly surrender her own body to her husband. She does not have to wait for explicit instructions. Instead, she can attempt to anticipate the commands. In order to do that, she needs intimate understanding of her husband's intentions, desires, goals, body, and other matters that may come into play. Of course, she also obeys him when he gives explicit instructions. Attempting to anticipate the commands does not entitle her to disobey any instructions that are given or substitute any action with her own in order to achieve her own desire or goal. Submission of the church to Jesus is an excellent example to illustrate these points.

I had a rare opportunity to engage in a research project in a university in Georgia pertaining to the training of military leaders. A couple of topics that constantly popped up during our discussions concerned the training of these future leaders for better decision making on the battlefield, where time is critical and short. To achieve the desired outcome requires extensive training in communication and engaging in drills to the point that executing a command and responding to a situation become second nature. It involves a coordinated effort of the whole platoon or team subjecting to the commands of its leader and executing them perfectly and without hesitation.

The submissiveness of a wife is not a matter of mere drills and exercises. It is not like a robot's response to a command or a platoon's rigid execution of an order. In the eyes of God, the wife ranks equally with her husband, and yet she is to willingly submit herself to him in the union of two becoming one flesh, where he is the head and she is the body. They are no longer two bodies and two heads but one body and one head. Although physically they are still two people, the couple acts as though they are only one head and one body. The head takes the lead, and the body acts in unison, even as the head serves the body.

The Love Mission

The love between husbands and wives has a common goal: their preparation to be the bride of Christ. Jesus himself has given husbands the example for how to be the head by showing us how he led the disciples and leads the church; and he has given wives the example for how to be the body by showing us how he submits himself to God the Father. God has created the unique institution of marriage between husbands and wives, whereby the husband is the head and the wife is the body. The sexual union of oneness is unique to humans, as are the roles of husband and wife in this sexual union. It is not a matter of equality or inequality in the roles. They are simply different. And the differences are necessary if we are to know how much God loves us and wants us to love him. He loved us so much that he was willing to sacrifice his treasured Son. We cannot love him by doing the same because we have nothing to offer him that he does not have. We owe our lives to Jesus because he redeemed us from the death sin brings. Our lives belong to him. Isn't it logical and natural that submission of our lives to him is the best way to show him our love?

The bond between husband and wife is built via sexual union, whereas the bond between Jesus and the church is built via spiritual union. Paul said this is a great mystery! Indeed, it is. Despite advances in the sciences, we still do not understand much about how the bond between husband and wife actually works. Agur, the son of Jakeh, expressed his wonder at the marvel of the sexual union:

> *There are three things which are too wonderful for me, yea, four which I know not: The way of an eagle in the air; the way of a serpent upon a rock; the way of a ship in the midst of the sea; and the way of a man with a maiden.*
> *Proverbs 30:18–19*

After three thousand years, we are still seeking to know more about this sexual union, not to mention the spiritual union with Jesus. No wonder Agur marveled. No wonder the apostle Paul said it is a great mystery (Ephesians 5:31–32).

Jesus loves us and has a great plan for us to reestablish the intimate bond with God. Instead of trying to imitate God at the spiritual level, Paul says we can imitate God through the roles husbands and wives play. Thus, if a husband plays the role God has assigned to him and a wife plays the role God has assigned to her, then the husband can imitate the love of Jesus, and the wife can imitate the love of the church.

Thus, the husband must be prepared to serve the needs of his wife. Here, of course, we are talking about the needs within the confines of the bedroom, recalling that both husband and wife are equally responsible for the daily needs of the family. By submitting to her husband, the wife is in a better position to learn how to submit to Jesus. By observing how his wife submits to him, the husband also benefits by learning how to submit himself to Jesus. By playing the leading role, the husband learns how to lead and understands better the expectations of Jesus. By observing her husband playing the leading role, the wife also benefits by learning to respond to his lead and to proactively engage in the love expressed by her husband.

It is a common idea that God joins a male and female in matrimony. God does not. We have to make our own decision, just as in everything else. God did not force Adam or Eve into matrimony. God merely brought Eve to Adam in the garden. It was Adam who desired Eve. It was Eve who did not reject Adam. Marriage is not created in heaven but made on earth.

In Genesis 24 there is a beautiful and, I think, romantic story about how Isaac found his wife. After Isaac's mother, Sarah, died at age 127, Abraham ordered his chief servant to go back to his home village to search for a wife for his son Isaac. In those days it was customary for people to travel in groups with servants who were able warriors because of the high risk of robbery, murder, and rape. This was also why females normally would have a male guardian, even though this was not a law or commandment in the Bible. After a long journey, the chief servant arrived at Nahor by a well, where he met Rebekah, the future wife of Isaac. Rebekah's guardian was her brother, since her father had passed away. It is interesting to note that her brother asked her opinion with regard to whether she would want the marriage, and she agreed to it, even though she had not met her future husband yet. Meanwhile, Isaac was waiting on his father's farm until the chief servant came back and explained to him all that had happened. He gladly accepted Rebekah as his wife. It appeared to be an arranged marriage, but with willing participants. This is an excellent example of a marriage made on earth. There was no "try before you buy." There was no dating. There was no celebration or partying. There was no wedding rituals or exchange of vows in the temple either. It was a simple marriage made to last the whole life. I do not mean that we should follow the example set down by Isaac and Rebekah. By all means, celebrate if one wishes to. The gist is that it is up to the individuals to make a happy marriage happen.

Jesus came into this world to repair the spiritual damage, redeem us from death, and reestablish our spiritual bond with God. The reestablishment of this bond can happen only if we decide to believe in Jesus and accept him into our lives. In the eyes of Jesus, all those who do this (that is, Christians) are his "flesh and bones" because the Holy Spirit is in them. Being the flesh and bones of Jesus ties in with the fact that we are his bride and we will be seen as such when he comes again.

> *There came unto me one of the seven angels who had the seven bowls full of the seven last plagues,*

> *and talked with me, saying, Come here, I will show you the bride, the Lamb's wife.*
> *Revelation 21:9*

Revelation is the last book of the Bible. In it the apostle John recorded what he was shown regarding the events that are going to happen in the future. And here we see the church as the bride of the Lamb. The Lamb refers to Jesus. So we have the first Eve born out of the physical, earthly Adam, and the last "Eve," the church, born out of the spiritual Jesus.

Originally, Adam and Eve had a spiritual connection with God.

> *The LORD God formed man of the dust of the ground, and breathed into his nostrils the breath of life; and man became a living soul.*
> *Genesis 2:7*

However, because of their disobedience, this connection was severed. Jesus provided for the reestablishment of this spiritual connection by sacrificing his own life. Now whoever accepts his free gift of redemption has eternal life and a spiritual relationship with God. Without this spiritual connection, we are "aliens" to God and not members of his family.

> *But you are not in the flesh, but in the Spirit, if so be that the Spirit of God dwells in you. Now if any man have not the Spirit of Christ, he is none of his. . . .*

> *For as many as are led by the Spirit of God, they are the sons of God.*
> *Romans 8:9, 14*

Although our spirit is made anew when we receive Christ, we are still not perfect. There is an ongoing process of sanctification we must embrace so that we may grow in spirit and be ready to be the bride of Jesus.

God establishes and sanctifies the unique, holy matrimonial union between a husband and a wife, and through this we are able to understand and appreciate God's divine Love. In the eyes of God, the sexual union between a man and a woman establishes them as husband and wife, which is very different from the contemporary legal definition of marriage. Marital sex is holy; and the roles of husbands and wives are clearly and divinely defined, and they are not interchangeable.

Naturally, as their love for God increases, the love between the spouses also increases. Similarly, as their love for one another increases, their love for God also increases. This is so because their love is built on the foundation laid down by God.

The world's wisest man, King Solomon, summarizes this three-tiered relationship:

> *Two are better than one; because they have a good reward for their labor. For if they fall, the one will lift up his fellow: but woe to him that is alone when he falls; for he has not another to help him up.*

Again, if two lie together, then they have heat: but how can one be warm alone? And if one prevails against him, two shall withstand him; and a threefold cord is not quickly broken.
Ecclesiastes 4:9–12

A person living alone could easily fall into Satan's trap and have no one to readily turn to for aid. Husband and wife can rely on one another to fend off the temptations of Satan. Add God to this sexual relationship, and they have a strong defense against Satan's attacks.

Summary

Right from the beginning of creation, God has had a grand, master plan to show and share his divine love for us. In fact, the whole Bible is about this divine love.

God created humans in his image and likeness. Being created in his image gives us superior features and allows us to dominate and control all other creatures. His likeness provides us with the more "humane" qualities that are unique to humans. However, due to the Fall, this godly image and likeness have been severely damaged. Even so, we still retain some of these characteristics that make us superior to other creatures. We still have our humane side.

We have discussed at length the two love relationships that mirror each another—one spiritual and one in physical, earthly flesh. It is through the earthly love between husband and wife that we begin to appreciate the divine love between Christ and his church; and all who believe in Jesus for salvation through his blood (i.e., Christians) are members of this church. Still, there are some, like the apostle Paul, who can fully grasp and understand this divine love, while being unmarried and celibate.

In God's master plan of love, the husband plays the role of the head and the wife that of the body, even as the two have become one flesh. Being the head, the husband is to love his wife, sacrifice for her in love, nurture and cherish her, and treat her as if she is his very flesh. As the body, the wife is to submit to her husband. Outwardly, it is important that she be obedient to him if the local customs and practices demand it. In this modern era, this may not be applicable except in some isolated areas or countries. In the bedroom, however, by God's designation of her role, she is to be submissive to her husband.

From the wife's role of submissiveness, both spouses benefit by learning how to submit to Jesus. From the husband's leading role, both also benefit by better understanding Jesus' love and his commandments. Their love grows because their love is built on the foundation of head and body, as laid down by God.

CHAPTER 4

Spiritual Maturity and Multiplication (Circumcision)

"I am the Almighty God; walk before me, and be you perfect. And I will make my covenant between me and you, and will multiply you exceedingly . . . you shall be a father of many nations. Neither shall your name any more be called Abram, but your name shall be Abraham; for a father of many nations have I made you. And I will make you exceedingly fruitful, and I will make nations of you, and kings shall come out of you. . . . As for Sarai your wife, you shall not call her name Sarai, but Sarah shall her name be. And I will bless her, and give you a son also of her: yea, I will bless her, and she shall be a mother of nations; kings of people shall come from her."
Genesis 17:1–2, 4–6, 15–16

As we have sought to discover the secrets of the first love, we learned in the previous chapter that the *sacrifice* of the husband and the *submission* of the wife, properly understood, are basic. Jesus' relationship to the church is the pattern for the husband-and-wife relationship. Before that, in chapter 2, we learned that *obedience* to God's commands is essential. Of particular note was God's command to Adam and Eve to multiply. This command was about earthly, physical survival. In this chapter we will show that there is a connection between physical, earthly *multiplication* and spiritual *multiplication*. By spiritual multiplication, we mean the multiplication of believers for the kingdom of God, which is the result of the process of *spiritual growth* and *maturity*. Interestingly enough, this spiritual work, which is another key to a fulfilling, God-honoring marriage, is connected to the physical act of circumcision.

Spiritual Survival and Multiplication

In the parable of the sower in Matthew 13, Jesus warns that if we do not persevere in building our bond with God, we soon will find ourselves being robbed of this bond by the world's temptations and our enemies.

> *Behold, a sower went forth to sow; And when he sowed, some seeds fell by the wayside, and the fowls came and devoured them up: Some fell upon*

> *stony places, where they had not much earth: and immediately they sprung up, because they had no deepness of earth: And when the sun was up, they were scorched; and because they had no root, they withered away. And some fell among thorns; and the thorns sprung up, and choked them: But others fell into good ground, and brought forth fruit, some a hundredfold, some sixtyfold, some thirtyfold.*
> *Matthew 13:3–8*

The seed is the gospel message of the kingdom of God. The soils represent various kinds of people who hear the gospel and respond to it in different ways. The wayside represents those who listen to the message but do not understand it. They are easily swayed by temptations, materialism, and others' opinions and quickly reject the gospel. The stony places are those who listen and readily accept the message. However, they are not rooted in the truth, and they turn away when trials come. The thorns represent people who hear the message and consider it, but they succumb to the allure of the world and all it promises; and eventually they go back to their old ways. Even if they do not deny Christianity, they never bear any spiritual fruit. The good ground represents people who accept the message. It takes root and grows in their lives. They genuinely believe the message, and they produce the fruit of righteousness and obedience.

The point is, we need to grow from a seed into a tree and bear fruit. In other words, we need to grow to spiritual maturity. The Bible often uses fruit as a metaphor for the different characteristics or attributes a Christian can and should possess. In Galatians, the apostle Paul presents a list of "fruits of the Holy Spirit" to describe the Christ-like attributes of a true Christian life.

The fruit of the Spirit is love, joy, peace, longsuffering [patience], gentleness, goodness, faith, Meekness, self-control: against such there is no law.

Galatians 5:22–23

The apostle Peter refers to these desirable virtues in the following way:

And for this reason, giving all diligence, add to your faith virtue; and to virtue knowledge; And to knowledge self control; and to self control patience; and to patience godliness; And to godliness brotherly kindness; and to brotherly kindness love.
2 Peter 1:5–7

Both apostles are saying that Christians should grow and bear fruit. It is this fruit that is a measure of their spiritual maturity. In fact, Jesus refers to himself as the vine and to Christians as the branches, and he expects the branches to bear fruit.

I am the true vine, and my Father is the vine dresser. Every branch in me that bears not fruit he takes away: and every branch that bears fruit, he prunes it, that it may bring forth more fruit.
John 15:1–2

That he is the vine and we are the branches makes sense, because it parallels the idea that he is the head and we are the body. It follows, then, that as long as the branches remain attached to the vine, the branches can draw nutrients from the vine and grow.

However, God is not concerned only about our growing and bearing fruit as individuals. He is also concerned about the growth and maturity of the church as a whole. For the church as a body to function and grow, it needs a whole range of abilities, or gifts, spread among its members. God knows what is best for each individual and the church as a whole, and he gives his children spiritual gifts accordingly. Not every Christian has the same gift, just as not every part of the body performs the same function (1 Corinthians 12:14–26). Each member is independent, and yet all members are interdependent and must work together for the growth and proper functioning of the whole body.

> *Speaking the truth in love, may [we] grow up into him in all things, who is the head, even Christ: From whom the whole body being fitly joined together and knit together by that which every joint supplies, according to the effectual working in the measure of every part, makes increase of the body unto the edifying of itself in love.*
> *Ephesians 4:15–16*

What are the God-given gifts? There are many. Paul lists some in 1 Corinthians.

> *But the manifestation of the Spirit is given to every man for profit. For to one is given by the Spirit the word of wisdom; to another the word of knowledge by the same Spirit; To another faith by the same Spirit; to another the gifts of healing by the same Spirit; To another the working of miracles; to another prophecy; to another discerning of spirits; to another various kinds of tongues; to another the interpretation of tongues. . . . And God has set some in the church, first apostles, secondarily prophets, thirdly teachers, after that miracles, then gifts of healings, helpers, administrators, various kinds of tongues.*
> 1 Corinthians 12:7-10, 28

It is quite clear that not every member will possess all these gifts. Each member must work in coordination with others, each using his or her individual gift for the good of the body.

Bearing fruit, and exercising the spiritual gifts God has given, prepares Christians to *multiply,* as we have been called to do. That is, we are to increase the number of Christians by introducing Jesus to unbelievers. After his resurrection, Jesus gave this command to his disciples:

> *Go you into all the world, and preach the gospel to every creature.*
> Mark 16:15

> *All power is given unto me in heaven and in earth. Go you therefore, and teach all nations, baptizing them in the name of the Father, and of the Son, and*

> *of the Holy Spirit: Teaching them to observe all things whatsoever I have commanded you: and, lo, I am with you always, even unto the end of the world. Amen.*
> *Matthew 28:18–20*

As the body of Christ, we are to submit ourselves to him. He is our commander, and it is the undeniable duty of every member of his body to fulfill his commands. Just like a submissive wife, we are to proactively engage in activities that will fulfill his commands and please him.

Sometimes we might unconsciously think that the Lord is a hard master. Like the servant in the parable of the pounds, we are ready to say, "For I feared you, because you are a severe man: you take up what you laid not down, and reap what you did not sow" (Luke 19:21). The motivation in such a case is fear, not love—we serve God because we are afraid of punishment if we do not serve him. That is a master-and-slave relationship, not a head-and-body relationship. Pleasing God should come to us naturally, from the bottom of our hearts, as willing submission to him in the fulfillment of his commands.

Jesus commands us as Christians to love God and to love our neighbors (Mark 12:30–31). If we truly love our neighbors, it follows that we should tell them the good news of Jesus and seek to bring them into Jesus' great spiritual family. This is so important that Jesus specifically commands us to spread the gospel.

And what, exactly, is the gospel? First Corinthians 15:3–4 provides a good summary of what the gospel is about.

> *For I [Paul] delivered unto you first of all that which I also received, how that Christ died for our sins according to the scriptures; And that he was buried, and that he rose again the third day according to the scriptures.*
> *1 Corinthians 15:3–4*

The gospel is the good news of the death, burial, and resurrection of Jesus Christ, which provide humanity full and free deliverance from the consequences of sins through faith in Christ. Humanity became separated from God when Adam and Eve disobeyed him and ate the fruit from the Tree of Knowledge of Good and Evil. This separation is termed sin. In order to reconcile people to God and reestablish the original relationship, God the Son, Jesus, became a man, though without sin. He ultimately died on the cross and bore the consequences of our sins. He was buried and descended to hell, but as the holy and righteous Son of God, he was resurrected. To anyone who accepts him as Savior, he gives the gift of a new spiritual life. This gift is free. We cannot give anything in exchange for it because it is priceless.

> *That if you shall confess with your mouth the Lord Jesus, and shall believe in your heart that God has raised him from the dead, you shall be saved.*
> *Romans 10:9*

> *Therefore as by the offence of one judgment came upon all men to condemnation; even so by the righteousness of one the free gift came upon all men unto justification of life.*
> *Romans 5:18*

We receive this free gift from Jesus by faith alone. He says,

> *Behold, I stand at the door, and knock: if any man hears my voice, and opens the door, I will come in to him, and will eat with him, and he with me.*
> *Revelation 3:20*

He knocks at the door of our hearts, and he promises to come and reside in and guide every person who opens the door. Jesus showed us his love by making the ultimate sacrifice of his life for us. The only proper way to respond to his love is to accept his gift of salvation. We can receive this salvation only by faith and faith alone. Good works will not satisfy the high standards demanded by God the Father, as set forth in the Ten Commandments. We all come short of his glory. As we mentioned before, Jesus came into this world to fulfill the requirements of the commandments and pay the penalty they required for our sins. Hence, only he can redeem us. All we need to do is repent of our sins and receive this free gift of redemption from Jesus. By repenting and accepting Jesus as our Savior, we are saying that we want to change from our old way of life and embrace the new way, the godly way. The Bible says that as a result we become a new creation.

> *Therefore if any man be in Christ, he is a new creation: old things are passed away; behold, all things are become new.*
> *2 Corinthians 5:17*

Jesus will live in us and give us a totally new outlook on life. We will desire to love and serve him and others.

> *For, brethren, you have been called unto liberty; only use not liberty for an occasion to the flesh, but by love serve one another. For all the law is fulfilled in one word, even in this; You shall love your neighbor as yourself.*
> *Galatians 5:13–14*

Our desire to love and please God is revealed by our obedience to his commands (John 14:15, 21). As we noted earlier, Christians are still called to obey the Ten Commandments. However, Jesus summarized the Ten Commandments into two. It is as we observe these two love commandments that we fulfill God's plan for us.

> *You shall love the Lord your God with all your heart, and with all your soul, and with all your mind. This is the first and great commandment. And the second is like unto it, You shall love your neighbor as yourself. On these two commandments hang all the law and the prophets [i.e., Ten Commandments].*
> *Matthew 22:37–40*

Nobody can find lasting satisfaction in life apart from a relationship with God—trusting Jesus Christ as Savior, obeying him, and growing toward spiritual maturity. Likewise, no couple can find lasting satisfaction in marriage apart from knowing, loving, and following Christ.

Origin of Spiritual Multiplication

The command to *multiply* in faith (that is, spiritually *multiply*) has its origin in Abraham, the "father of faith." Abraham was originally called Abram. He came from the land of Ur of the Chaldeans (Genesis 11:28). Abraham's father, Terah, took Abraham and his wife Sarai, who was later renamed Sarah, along with Abraham's nephew Lot, and travelled as far as Haran, where they settled. After Terah died, God instructed Abraham to leave Haran and go to the place he would show him. There, God promised, he would make Abraham a great nation and through him bring blessing to the entire earth.

> *Now the LORD had said unto Abram, Get you out of your country, and from your kindred, and from your father's house, unto a land that I will show you: And I will make of you a great nation, and I will bless you, and make your name great; and you shall be a blessing: And I will bless them that bless you, and curse him that curses you: and in you shall all families of the earth be blessed.*
> *Genesis 12:1–3*

In obedience to God's call, Abraham took his wife, Sarah, and nephew Lot and journeyed to Shechem in Canaan. There, God appeared to Abraham and confirmed that this land was his inheritance. Abraham did not immediately inherit the land, though. In fact, soon afterward, he went to Egypt to escape a severe famine. From there he returned to Canaan, bringing with him great riches and many possessions. Sometime later, Abraham encountered God again, and God reassured Abraham that his descendants would multiply into an innumerable people who would inherit the great land of Canaan:

> *For all the land which you see, to you will I give it, and to your descendants forever. And I will make your descendants as the dust of the earth.*
> *Genesis 13:15–16*

Through the years Abraham and Sarah surely tried to make sense of how he would become a progenitor of nations, when it seemed impossible for them to have children. After living in Canaan for ten years and still with no child, Sarah suggested that Abraham could fulfill God's promise of having a son through her maid, Hagar. This resulted in the birth of Ishmael and a fiery relationship between Sarah and Hagar.

Abraham learned many lessons of faith during his long life. In some cases he passed the test; in other cases his faith seemed to be wanting. Nevertheless, the Bible recounts his progress in faith and obedience to God.

Finally, at age ninety-nine, twenty-four years after Abraham came to the Promised Land and thirteen years after Hagar gave birth to Ishmael, God appeared to Abraham and declared that he would be the "father of many nations."

> *And when Abram was ninety years old and nine, the LORD appeared to Abram, and said unto him, I am the Almighty God; walk before me, and be you perfect. And I will make my covenant between me and you, and will multiply you exceedingly. And Abram fell on his face: and God talked with him, saying, As for me, behold, my covenant is with you, and you shall be a father of many nations. . . . And I will make you exceedingly fruitful, and I will make nations of you, and kings shall come out of you. And I will establish my covenant between me and you and your descendants after you in their generations for an everlasting covenant, to be a God unto you, and to your descendants after you. And I will give unto you, and to your descendants after you, the land in which you are a sojourner, all the land of Canaan, for an everlasting possession; and I will be their God. And God said unto Abraham, You shall keep my covenant therefore, you, and your descendants after you in their generations. This is my covenant, which you shall keep, between me and you and your descendants after you; Every male child among you shall be circumcised. And you shall circumcise the flesh of your foreskins; and it shall be a sign of the covenant between me and you. And he that is eight days old shall be circumcised among you. . . . And God said unto Abraham, As for Sarai your wife,*

you shall not call her name Sarai, but Sarah shall her name be. And I will bless her, and give you a son also of her: yea, I will bless her, and she shall be a mother of nations; kings of people shall come from her.
Genesis 17:1-4, 6-12, 15–16

In Genesis 17 God reaffirmed the covenant he made with Abraham in Genesis 15. Abraham had faithfully obeyed his command to uproot from one place and settle in another. Although at times Abraham had doubts about how the different pieces fit together, he nevertheless remained faithful. Although he did not know how to handle certain situations and at times feared for his life, never once did he turn away from God. Despite the dangers and difficulties along the journey, he believed and trusted God; and by faith in God, he was declared righteous before God (Genesis 15:6). As a sign of the covenant and of his faith in God, Abraham was given circumcision as a practice to be observed perpetually by his descendants.

The following year, Sarah indeed gave birth to a son, Isaac. And even after Isaac's birth, God tested the faith of Abraham once more, when he commanded Abraham to take his only son to a certain place and sacrifice him on an altar (Genesis 22). Once again, Abraham showed his total commitment to trust and serve God. That famous story of the "sacrifice" of his son Isaac foreshadows the sacrifice of Jesus, which purchased salvation for all who trust in him.

It was because of Abraham's righteousness as a result of his faith that God could call him to walk before God (Genesis 17:1). "Walk before Me," or "stand before Me," means to serve God. God's promise, or covenant, to bless Abraham and give him countless descendants called for continuing faith and faithfulness on Abraham's part. It also called for a physical sign that God's promise was being passed on from generation to generation. That sign was circumcision.

The Hebrew word for "male" in Genesis 17:10 is *zakar* (*zaw-kawr'*), which is derived from the word meaning "to remember." In the Jewish tradition, the male Jew has the obligation of remembering and transmitting the traditions from father to son. The male Jew is reminded of the Abrahamic covenant by the sign of the covenant: circumcision. The covenant serves as a reminder of Abraham's trust in God and determination to serve him.

On the other hand, Sarah needs no circumcision. In the Jewish tradition, it is the mother who conveys the Jewish status and birthright to her child,[22] guaranteeing the future of the entire Jewish people. Genesis 17:15 implies that Sarah was the very embodiment of the covenant and in reality is the "mother of nations" (verse 16). God never requires a female to be circumcised.

God made it clear that to be a physical heir to the covenant, one needs to be a descendant of Abraham *and* Sarah. Thus, Isaac, the son of Abraham and Sarah, inherited the covenant promises. His half-brother Ishmael, the son of Abraham and Hagar, did not.

And as for Ishmael, I [God] have heard you [Abraham]: Behold, I have blessed him, and will make him fruitful, and will multiply him exceedingly; twelve princes shall he beget, and I will make him a great nation. But my covenant will I establish with Isaac, whom Sarah shall bear unto you at this set time in the next year.
Genesis 17:20–21

An interesting point to note is that, although all Jews and Arabs today trace their ancestry to him, Abraham himself was neither a Jew nor an Arab. The term *Jew* comes from the name Judah, one of the twelve sons of Jacob, the son of Isaac. As it is used today, it refers to the descendants of Abraham and Sarah.

As we consider the events that led to the first biblical circumcision, we should note that as Abraham grew in faith, God's promise to him grew as well. First, God promised to make him a great nation and give him the land called Canaan (Genesis 12:1–3). Then God extended the promise to his descendants (Genesis 12:7), promising that his posterity would be innumerable (Genesis 13:16). Finally, God reaffirmed that Abraham's descendants would come directly from his flesh (Genesis 15:4).

We often overlook Abraham's faith in relation to his nephew Lot. As the two journeyed through the land, strife arose between Abraham's herdsmen and Lot's because the land could not provide sufficiently for their vast herds. So they amicably decided to go their separate ways. Lot chose to live in the land that seemed best, but it was near Sodom, which the Bible describes as a wicked city where the dwellers indulged in perverse sexual practices. Abraham chose to dwell in Hebron in the south and built an altar to worship God there (Genesis 13:5–18). His wise choice to trust in God and obey his commands rather than selfishly seek material wealth demonstrated his faith in God and the everlasting covenant that was marked by circumcision.

Thus, although circumcision is merely a symbolic token, it signifies a significant covenant between God and the bearer of the token, and the obligation to remain faithful to God in carrying out the duty to serve him. God's promise of blessings, in fact, reaches beyond Abraham's descendants to all nations. Indeed, Christians look to Abraham as the father of all who believe (Romans 4:11).

When Moses wrote the book of Deuteronomy, God inspired him to put side by side the Mosaic laws and the theme of love (cf. Deuteronomy 6:5; 7:6–9; 10:12, 18; 11:1, 13, 22; 13:3; 19:9; 30:6, 16, 20). Why would love be such a major element in the law? Moses wrote the book to prepare the new generation of Israelites to enter the Promised Land of Canaan. He recounted the nation's journey out of Egypt, the failings of the people, God's blessings, and the laws God gave them, including, of course, the Ten Commandments. He then announced to the people that they were about to enter the Promised Land and that God would *circumcise* their hearts.

> *And the LORD your God will bring you into the land which your fathers possessed, and you shall possess it; and he will do you good, and multiply*

you above your fathers. And the LORD your God will circumcise your heart, and the heart of your descendants, to love the LORD your God with all your heart, and with all your soul, that you may live.
Deuteronomy 30:5–6

However, immediately upon entering the Promised Land, God commanded Moses' successor, Joshua, to perform Abrahamic circumcision.

At that time the LORD said unto Joshua, Make you sharp knives, and circumcise again the children of Israel the second time. . . . Now all the people that came out were circumcised: but all the people that were born in the wilderness by the way as they came forth out of Egypt, them they had not circumcised.
Joshua 5:2, 5

The Israelites of this new generation were to be leaders and to serve God. Performing Abrahamic circumcision was required, following God's covenant with Abraham. But why did Moses say, "The Lord your God will circumcise your heart"? Why did God instruct Moses to tell the Israelites one thing and instruct Joshua to do another? It seems God wanted his people to understand the true meaning of circumcision. It is not the outward act but the inner reality that it reflects that is important. Paul wrote,

> *For in Jesus Christ neither circumcision avails anything, nor uncircumcision; but faith which works by love.*
> *Galatians 5:6*

When Moses told the people about circumcision of the heart, he also urged them to love God, with the famous commandment of love. Circumcision of the heart is about loving God. It is spiritual love.

> *Love the LORD your God with all your heart, and with all your soul, that you may live.*
> *Deuteronomy 30:6*

Sacrificial love comes from the heart, mind, and soul, not from following a list of things to do. Through the prophet Moses, God reminds us that physical circumcision is meaningless apart from circumcision of the heart—the love that gives without reservation. God has made physical circumcision a reminder to the bearer of the mark of the duty and commitment to love God unreservedly.

The question, then, is this: Why did God choose to put the mark on the most intimate part? God easily could have put a mark on the forehead, in the earlobe, on the nose, or on any other part of the body. The Bible does not provide any clear answer or clue—at least not that I know of. However, the very fact that it is marked on the intimate part gives us the strongest hint that it relates to intimate love.

We recall that God called Abraham to be circumcised for a specific purpose—to commit himself to serve him and to lead the multitudes of his people. From the life of Abraham, we see that he in fact obeyed God's commandments. Yes, his faith faltered on occasion, but he did not give up his willingness to carry out the divine duties. He faced many challenges, but he persevered in fulfilling God's commandments to him. His journey into Egypt when there was a famine, his split with his nephew Lot because of their vast herds, the courageous rescue of Lot, his bold appeal to the angry God to spare the righteous in Sodom, and his subsequent acceptance of God's decision to destroy the cities of Sodom and Gomorrah—all these show his intimate relationship with God and his commitment to serve him. Ultimately, when faced with the challenge of choosing between his only begotten son, Isaac, and obedience to God, he showed his wholehearted devotion and unreserved consecration to God, even to the point of being willing to sacrifice his son.

Faith in God, loving and serving God, and commitment to spiritually multiplying his followers by passing the faith on to others—all these ideas are wrapped up in the concept of spiritual "circumcision of the heart." Regardless of the presence or absence of physical circumcision, which symbolizes them, these are the qualities that are to be present in the lives of all Christians. It is fair to say, then, that circumcision of the heart is one of the key secrets to the first love and essential to lasting, satisfying marriages.

Secrets of First Love

Physical Circumcision

At this point we want to step aside and take some time to consider physical circumcision in the Bible, history, and culture. This is important for several reasons. First, physical circumcision is a prominent topic in both the Old and New Testaments. Second, it has some bearing on physical intimacy in marriage. And, third, as we have seen, it has important value as a symbol of the far more significant circumcision of the heart.

MALE CIRCUMCISION

The origin of male circumcision cannot be known with certainty. Although the oldest records of circumcision perhaps come from Egypt,[23] many cultures throughout the world have practiced circumcision at some point in their history. This includes the Arabic countries, Israel,[24] Australia,[25] Canada, United States of America, South Africa, New Zealand, United Kingdom, Timor, Indonesia,[26] the Philippines,[27] and the Polynesian Islands.[28] The reasons for the practice of circumcision vary widely. Some suggest it started as a religious ritual for a boy passing into manhood and was a demonstration of one's ability to endure pain.[29] Others suggest it was originally practiced for hygienic reasons, where regular bathing was impractical,[30] or as a means of prevention of or protection against certain infections.[31] Still others propose that it was a sign of fertility or a means of demarcation of a higher social status. There is also the suggestion it was meant as a means of discouraging masturbation,[32] although this claim is suspect.[33]

When God made the covenant with Abraham, the practice of circumcision obviously existed already. Abraham might have acquired knowledge of circumcision in Egypt. Indeed, God often uses what is prevailing as an emblem of his promise. This was the case when God promised Noah he would never destroy the human race again by flood and established the rainbow as the sign of that covenant (Genesis 9:13). Jewish circumcision may well have been borrowed from the Egyptians;[34] however, the circumcision Abraham performed was different from that practiced in Egypt.[35] The Egyptians removed the whole prepuce (foreskin),[36] thus exposing the whole glans (head) of the penis. The word *circumcise* in Hebrew is *mul* (*mool*), which means to blunt, curtail, or cut short. Thus, Abrahamic circumcision removed only the "excess" foreskin protruding beyond the tip of the organ. This circumcision is called *milah,* and the procedure was applied to eight-day-old baby boys. Only the tip of a newborn's foreskin hanging past the end of the shaft was clipped off. We witness this when Moses' wife Zipporah circumcised her son. She used a flint stone to perform the procedure. She surely did not perform the very risky Egyptian-style circumcision, removing the entire foreskin with a flint and doing it in a hurry.

> *And it came to pass by the way in the inn, that the LORD met him [Moses], and sought to kill him. Then Zipporah took a sharp stone, and cut off the foreskin of her son, and cast it at his feet, and said,*

> *Surely a bloody husband are you to me. So he let him go: then she said, A bloody husband you are, because of the circumcision.*
> *Exodus 4:24–26*

Moses fled from Egypt because he had killed an Egyptian. Later God called him to lead the Israelites out of Egypt. Eventually Moses accepted God's calling and journeyed back to Egypt. It was on this journey that he encountered God again. This time, however, God wanted to kill him. Why did God want to kill Moses? The Bible does not give a reason. However, we see that God's anger subsided due to the swift action of Zipporah circumcising her son using a flint stone. No doubt Moses and Zipporah had discussed Abrahamic circumcision; thus, she was fully aware of the meaning behind it and immediately sensed the reason Moses' God was angry.

Zipporah was not a Hebrew but a Midianite. Most scholars agree that the Midianites did not practice circumcision. It was obvious Zipporah didn't like circumcision, and this is probably the reason her son was not circumcised. Some scholars suggest Moses himself did not circumcise his son for her sake and that this was why she instinctively realized the cause of God's wrath: that Moses had failed to fulfill the obligation of the Abrahamic covenant. This view may be suggested from the fact that Zipporah hastily circumcised her son and cast the foreskin at Moses' feet and declared him "a bloody husband." The word for "feet" in Hebrew is *regel (reh'-gel)*, which may be a euphemism for the private parts. By touching Moses with the foreskin, she might have been implying that Moses also was not circumcised as yet and she was circumcising her son in his place. "So he let him go" also may imply that God allowed Moses to go without being circumcised. As we will learn later, lack of circumcision is not a sin.

The Jews routinely performed Abrahamic circumcision, or *brit milah,* and this set them apart from their neighbors clear through the era of Jesus Christ.[37] The Bible records that Jesus was circumcised on the eighth day after his birth (Luke 2:21), following the Abrahamic tradition. The first generation of Christians were Jews and thus certainly were circumcised. However, as the churches expanded into Gentile areas, many non-Jews were converted. This became problematic, as some of the Jewish Christians insisted these Gentiles needed to conform to the Abrahamic covenant in order to be saved. Paul saw this as inconsistent with the teachings of Jesus and forcefully taught that circumcision contributed nothing toward salvation.

> *For in Christ Jesus neither circumcision avails anything, nor uncircumcision, but a new creation.*
> *Galatians 6:15*

Christians believe that through Jesus Christ's death, burial, and resurrection he has paid the penalty for our sins and provided eternal life through faith in him. Baptism is the symbol of his death, burial, and resurrection, and Jesus commands all Christians to be baptized as a symbol to the world and the angels that the old person has died and been buried and a new person has been reborn. Circumcision is not about salvation. It is about spiritual maturity and multiplication and loving and serving God. In that sense, it is not the same as the symbolism of baptism.

Abraham trusted God and believed his promise of a land and a multitude of descendants, and he committed himself to serve him. The author of Hebrews defines this trust and belief in God as "faith." It is this faith that earned Abraham the calling from God to serve before him and be the leader of God's people.

> *By faith Abraham, when he was called to go out into a place which he should later receive for an inheritance, obeyed; and he went out, not knowing where he went. By faith he sojourned in the land of promise, as in a foreign land, dwelling in tents with Isaac and Jacob, the heirs with him of the same promise: For he looked for a city which has foundations, whose builder and maker is Go*
> *Hebrews 11:8–10*

Circumcision is the sign of God's covenant promise to Abraham and his descendants and a reminder of Abraham's faith in that promise.

The faith of salvation is belief in Jesus and his promise to forgive one's sins. There are no good deeds to be performed on the part of the believer. Salvation is by grace alone. It is freely given to those who believe in Jesus.

Jesus came into this world and gave us the commandments of love. And those who are committed to obeying his new commandments are said to have circumcised hearts. The old commandments were engraved on stone tablets. The new commandments are written in our hearts.

Abraham was declared righteous (Genesis 15:6) *before* he was circumcised in the flesh (Genesis 17:23–25). So, it is clear that circumcision contributes nothing to salvation. It is rather a symbol of the covenant with Abraham. Baptism in the New Testament is not a replacement for circumcision of the Old Testament. They symbolize different realities.

> *How was it [blessings] then reckoned? when he [Abraham] was in circumcision, or in uncircumcision? Not in circumcision, but in uncircumcision. And he received the sign of circumcision, a seal of the righteousness of the faith which he had yet being uncircumcised: that he might be the father of all them that believe, though they be not circumcised; that righteousness might be imputed unto them also.*
> *Romans 4:10–11*

In the same manner, a Christian is declared righteous (when he or she believes in Jesus) before he or she is circumcised in the heart (i.e., learns to obey the commandments of love).

> *He is a Jew [child of Abraham], who is one inwardly; and circumcision is that of the heart, in the spirit, and not in the letter.*

Romans 2:29

Circumcision is not found in the Ten Commandments, and failure to practice circumcision is not a sin. Paul puts it this way:

> *Is any man called being circumcised? let him not become uncircumcised. Is any called in uncircumcision? let him not be circumcised. Circumcision is nothing, and uncircumcision is nothing, but the keeping of the commandments of God. Let every man abide in the same calling in which he was called.*
> *1 Corinthians 7:18–20*

In other words, Paul is effectively saying that if we who are called to follow Christ want to be circumcised, we may do so. If we do not want to follow this practice, we are free not to. Excellent examples are found in the cases of Timothy and Titus. Timothy had a Jewish Christian mother and a Greek father, and Paul circumcised him (Acts 16:1–3). Titus was a Greek, and Paul did not circumcise him (Galatians 2:3). So, does that mean circumcision (and the covenant it symbolizes) is abolished? No, not so. For Paul also said,

> *For circumcision verily profits, if you keep the law: but if you are a breaker of the law, your circumcision is made uncircumcision.*
> *Romans 2:25*

Circumcision does have benefits under certain conditions. We will explore this idea later.

Circumcision has been, and continues to be, a divisive issue. There was much confusion early on surrounding the theological issue of whether Gentile converts to the Christian faith should be circumcised or not. A debate among the early Christians took place in Jerusalem (Acts 15). This meeting was largely held to clarify the reasons circumcision was not necessary for salvation. The debate went on for some time, and in the end James, the brother of Jesus, concluded thus:

> *Therefore my judgment is, that we trouble not them, who from among the Gentiles are turned to God.*
> *Acts 15:19*

A clear doctrine emerged that circumcision was not needed to complete salvation, as Paul states in Galatians.

> *For in Jesus Christ neither circumcision avails anything, nor uncircumcision; but faith which works by love.*
> *Galatians 5:6*

Faith here refers to belief in Jesus for salvation. The Bible never says one needs to be circumcised in order to be saved.

Christians were not obligated to perform circumcision. Meanwhile, the Jews continued with the *brit milah*[38] and developed a device called the barzel to safeguard the glans during circumcision.³⁹ Only the foreskin protruding beyond the glans, which was pulled through the slit in the device, was snipped off.

In the fourth century BC, Alexander the Great conquered the ancient Near East and introduced Greek customs and culture to the conquered lands. One of the cultural institutions he brought with him was the gymnasium. The Greeks did not circumcise and did their exercises in the gymnasium naked. When the Jews entered the gymnasium, they were embarrassed because their circumcision became apparent. To conform they underwent a decircumcision process (epispasm) to disguise their circumcision so that they appeared like Greeks.

By AD 140 Israel for the most part had assimilated the Greek culture in all walks of life. The Pharisees, however, continued to hold unwaveringly to the belief that to be a Jewish male meant being physically circumcised, and they could no longer tolerate the epispasm practices. They invented an elaborate procedure of circumcision called the *periah* so that the Jews could not hide their identity. After performing the *milah,* a second step, *periah,* was then performed. This consisted of tearing and stripping back the remaining inner mucosal lining of the foreskin from the glans of the infant boy and then, by use of a sharp fingernail or implement, removing all of the inner mucosal tissue, including the excising and removal of the frenulum from the underside of the glans. This was a significant departure from Abrahamic circumcision, having no biblical basis or command of God. Circumcision had lost its purpose. For the Jews who still insisted on the practice, it had become an emblem of pride in the Jewish race and had lost its spiritual meaning.

Christians continued to enjoy the free choice of either being circumcised or not. However, by the eighteenth and nineteenth centuries, circumcision among English-speaking countries such as the United States of America and Canada became common practice, made popular by physicians such as S. I. McMillen[40] and Peter Remondino.[41] The *periah* type of infant circumcision also became routine.[42] The arguments offered in support of it included prevention of habitual masturbation and various health and hygiene benefits, such as a nearly endless list of presumed cures for a variety of ailments and diseases,[43] as well as HIV prevention.[44] Another reason given was the attitude of peers and sons' self-esteem.[45] If the father is circumcised, it is more likely the son will be circumcised.[46]

Today the controversy over circumcision is even more polarized than ever, with pro- and anti- circumcision groups fiercely promoting their agendas. We should be aware that the two camps clearly are comparing uncircumcision with the *periah* type of circumcision, which is obviously different from God's sanctioned Abrahamic circumcision.

NEONATAL CIRCUMCISION

Infant circumcision inevitably becomes the focal point of the debate.[47] On one hand, we have many verses and examples in the Bible that seem to indicate infant circumcision is mandatory. In fact, God's commandment to Abraham clearly required circumcision on eight-day-old infant boys, and Jesus himself was circumcised on the eighth day. On the other hand, the anti-circumcision and human rights advocates of today are very vocal and vehement in their opposition to infant circumcision. They advocate that circumcision amounts to mutilation of a body part, and an infant should be entitled to decide for himself whether he wants to subject himself to this mutilation. Parents have no right to make such a drastic decision for him, they declare. In fact, the apostle Paul seems to call people who perform such *periah* circumcision mutilators.

> *Beware of dogs, beware of evil workers, beware of the mutilators.*
> *Philippians 3:2*

The infant circumcision currently performed in the United States of America and many parts of the world is similar to *periah* in that it involves removing the entire foreskin, exposing the entire glans permanently. Clearly this does not conform to the practice laid down in God's commandment to Abraham. (The author of this book holds the view that infant circumcision should not be performed anymore, but for a different reason.)

Circumcision performed by ancient Jews right up to the era of Jesus Christ was termed the *milah;* only the protruding tip of the prepuce was removed, and the glans remained covered. If infant circumcision is performed, then we need to conform to the *milah,* as this is the procedure sanctioned by God

We have learned that God commanded Abraham to circumcise all infant boys on the eighth day after birth (Genesis 17:12). In modern times it has been discovered that in a newborn child, vitamin K is produced from the fifth day and peaks on the eighth day after birth. This vitamin, together with prothrombin, a protein in the blood plasma, causes blood coagulation, which is important in any surgical procedure. Isabella Shepherd observed that for the first three days a newborn's prothrombin level actually falls to about 10 percent of that of an adult. After that, it increases and peaks after the seventh day.[48] Thus, the eighth day is the best time to perform a surgery such as circumcision.

Since this clinical observation matches God's commandment to circumcise an infant boy on the eighth day, I am inclined to hold the view that God knows what is best. In ancient times, when medical knowledge was limited, God stipulated the eighth day for infant circumcision, simply because that was the safest day. Male adult circumcision was symbolic of the commitment to serve God and lead his people. The divine intention of the symbolism was to remind the bearer of the symbol of his commitments to God. In return, God would *multiply* his descendants. The covenant was for eternity. Hence, it required the bearer to perpetuate the mark on the flesh from generation to generation, and the eighth day was the ideal and safest time to make the mark on a potential bearer while he was still an infant, as the risk of infection would be reduced to a minimum. With the advancement of medicine and technology, circumcision today presents only a very small risk for both adults and infants. In fact, it can be performed free of pain and bleeding.

As we have seen, circumcision, whether infant or adult, is unnecessary and largely meaningless today. More important for Christian parents is to teach their children so that they grow up maintaining their Christian faith. Circumcision on the father (rather than the child) may serve as a reminder in this respect of a commitment to God to serve him for life. But if it is optional for adults, it should not be routinely practiced on infants.

FEMALE CIRCUMCISION

All of this also raises the question of female circumcision. All physical circumcision mentioned in the Bible, however, concerns male circumcision. Females were not required to be circumcised.

Females (or wives) play a different role in the order of God's divine plan of love—the submissive role. In this role the wife accepts the love expressed by her husband. The wife responds and resonates the loving lead from the husband, just as the church responds to the love of Jesus. We, the church, submit to Jesus and commit ourselves to his commandments of love. We learn and strive to achieve all the virtues in the Bible such as love, joy, peace, longsuffering [perseverance], gentleness, goodness, faith, meekness, and self-control (Galatians 5:22–23). Sacrificial love is *giving* in love. Submissive love is *receiving* in love.

Another reason for not circumcising females is in the anatomy. If the female prepuce of the clitoris (which is similar to the foreskin of the male) is removed, the clitoris will be exposed to the harsh external environment. This will be apparent when we give a brief description of the male and female anatomies in the next chapter.

Summary

Abrahamic circumcision is a "mark in the flesh" whereby the male is reminded of his promise and commitment to God to serve him in fulfilling his commandment to *multiply*—both in the physical and the spiritual sense. Physical *multiplication* refers to God's promise to Abraham to greatly increase his descendants (Israelites) and perpetuate the inheritance of Israel as a nation. Spiritual *multiplication* foreshadows the multitudes of Christians who are born into the kingdom of God through Jesus Christ. Thus, Abraham is often referred to as the Father of the Jews, as well as the Father of Faith. From the story of Abraham in the book of Genesis, we observe that this *faith* refers to his trust in God.

Abrahamic circumcision is not a part of salvation. Paul conclusively states that salvation is not by deeds but by grace only. Every person has sinned, and the penalty for sin is death. There is no deed we can offer as redemption for our punishment. Only the sinless Jesus can redeem us with his own death. The Bible says the salvation he has purchased for us is free to all who will simply receive it by faith. Circumcision is a work of the flesh and has no part in salvation. It is simply a symbol, as is baptism—the former being a symbol of a commitment to serve God and multiply, and the latter being a symbol of having accepted the salvation of Jesus.

The conclusion from the debate in Jerusalem (Acts 15:5–11) was that circumcision is optional. This is not surprising, given that it has nothing to do with salvation. No two persons are the same. Not all Christians receive the same calling. Some are called to be pastors, some to be elders, some to be missionaries, and some to be evangelists. Some may want to commit to bearing the seal of the Abrahamic covenant; some may not. The apostle Paul viewed circumcision as a personal preference, even though he saw merit or benefits in it.

While we have taken much time in this chapter to look at physical circumcision, the real importance of this act was as a mark of God's covenant with Abraham and his descendants. It was a reminder of God's promise to multiply Abraham's family (i.e., the Hebrews or Jewish people), a mark of faith in God's promise, and a mark of love for God. This is why the Bible can also speak of *circumcision of the heart,* that is, a heart marked by love and faith in God and all his promises. Both circumcision of the flesh and circumcision of the heart have a bearing on marriage and the first love God established from the beginning. Physical circumcision reminds us that God's promises touch even the most intimate moments of married life, and spiritual circumcision reminds us that physical intimacy has little meaning apart from a genuine, growing, maturing faith, which is a crucial ingredient of the first love.

CHAPTER 5

Physical Intimacy: The Anatomy

And Adam said, This is now bone of my bones, and flesh of my flesh: she shall be called Woman, because she was taken out of Man. Therefore shall a man leave his father and his mother, and shall cleave unto his wife: and they shall be one flesh. Genesis 2:23–24

We have seen that obedience to God, sacrificial and submissive love, and a commitment to spiritual maturity and multiplication are key elements in the love relationship of husband and wife as God intended it. And we have seen how these crucial ingredients in marriage relate to creation, the order of creation, and circumcision. Throughout, we have hinted at another key, or "secret," of the love relationship: physical, or sexual, intimacy. This chapter and the two that follow focus on this aspect of love.

If we are to fully understand and appreciate the sexual aspect of marriage, we need to have some basic facts about the anatomy of the male and female organs and their functions. This is especially important in order to avoid some common misconceptions. Any helpful counsel on the physical relationship between husband and wife must include an explanation of these basic facts.

A look at the functions of the organs in sexual activities also ties in with our previous discussion of circumcision and will help us to dismiss the prevailing misconceptions and make a better decision whether to circumcise.

Finally, knowledge of male and female anatomy and functions will help us to understand the love story and lyrics in the book of Song of Songs, which we will study in chapter 7.

Secrets of First Love

Male Reproductive System

The male reproductive system consists of three basic organs.

The testicles (also called the gonads or sex glands)

The prostate gland and the seminal vesicles

The penis, with its glans and tissues

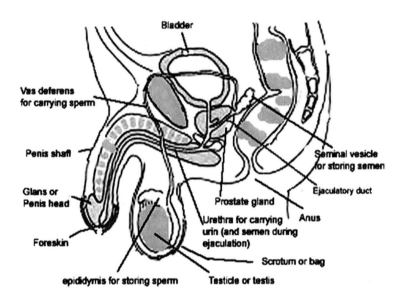

Side view of male reproductive system

TESTICLES

The two testicles are normally carried in the scrotum, which is also called the bag. Each testicle is about the size of the female ovary. This is where the male reproductive cells, called sperm cells, are produced. When the sperm reach maturity, they move into the tube called the epididymis, which forms as a bundle at the top end of the testicles.

During sexual excitement, the sperm are carried along the long tube called the vas deferens to the prostate gland. The vas from each testicle widens out just before it enters the prostate and joins into the pouch structure behind the prostate known as the seminal vesicle. This is where the sperm are stored.

PROSTATE

The prostate gland is located at the base of the urinary bladder, encircling the urethra and the bladder neck. In a young man, the prostate gland is about the size of a walnut. As a man ages, the prostate enlarges so that in his sixties and seventies it will normally be two or three times larger. Generally, this is not a problem unless the enlargement poses serious compression on the urethra, causing various degrees of urinary symptoms, such as a decreased stream or increased frequency and urgency of urination.

During sexual climax (ejaculation), the prostatic secretion and other secretions from the surrounding glands are added to form the seminal fluid in which the sperm can swim. The fluid, called the ejaculate or semen, is forced out from the seminal vesicles into the ejaculatory duct at the base of the penis. By a series of muscular contractions that take place in the prostate gland, the semen is expulsed through the urethra and out of the meatus or the outside opening of the urethra.

PENIS

The penis is comprised of what commonly is called the shaft or phallus, which forms the length of the penis, and the head, or glans. The shaft is made up of three columns of spongy, erectile tissue, two side by side and one at the bottom. The bottom one is softer, and the urethra passes through it. The urethra is a tube through which urine is passed under normal conditions. Semen also passes through it. During ejaculation, the semen travels through the ejaculatory ducts and mixes with fluids from the seminal vesicles, the prostate, and the other internal glands. It finally travels through the urethra and is ejected outside the body. The semen is a grayish-white bodily fluid that is secreted by the gonads and other internal glands in the male. It carries sperm, fructose, and other enzymes that help the sperm to survive and thus facilitate successful fertilization. The milky appearance is due to the large amount of sperm and proteins it carries.

The glans is very sensitive to touch. It contains many nerve endings that help build orgasmic tension during sexual activities. It is covered by a double-layered fold of skin called the prepuce, or foreskin.

The foreskin needs special attention to keep it hygienic and to prevent the accumulation of a greasy secretion called smegma.

Under normal conditions, the unstimulated penis is flaccid (or soft), and the glans remains covered with the foreskin. The inner layer of the foreskin is soft and thin, just like the skin inside the mouth. The outer layer is thicker. The inner foreskin contains many nerve endings that are sensitive to touch and pressure, although they are less sensitive than the glans. The inner foreskin joins to the shaft at the base of the glans, or corona ridge. It then extends from the corona ridge toward the tip of the penis, covering the whole glans, usually protruding beyond the tip of the glans. It then folds outwards and back to form the outer foreskin. This outer skin runs from the tip of the penis back to the base of the shaft, which joins to the body trunk at the base of the pubic bone. Thus, the glans is covered by the double-layered foreskin, whereas the shaft is covered by a single layer of the skin, known as the shaft skin.

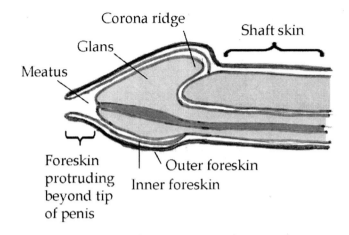

Flaccid penis (before circumcision)

During sexual arousal the penis is engorged with blood and expands, causing an erection. The foreskin then retracts to accommodate the extended penis. However, there is normally still enough foreskin to cover the glans so that the glans is exposed only slightly, if at all. In some cases, the foreskin retracts and forms a lump behind the glans. In most cases it is possible to pull the foreskin and cover over the glans. Besides the glans, sexual sensation also can be derived from the inner foreskin by folding and unfolding it.

Physical Intimacy: Anatomy

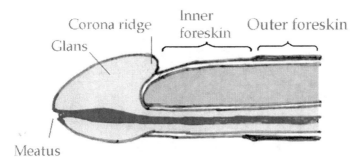

Circumcised penis (erect)

In the case of a man circumcised according to Abrahamic circumcision, or *milah*, the excess foreskin beyond the glans is removed, with the remaining foreskin just enough to cover the glans when it is flaccid. During sexual arousal, the extended penis causes the foreskin to unfold and retract. The result is that the soft, inner foreskin lines up along the upper part of the shaft with the glans fully exposed. The coronal ridge forms at the joint between the penis shaft and the glans, giving the glans the appearance of a mushroom head. The tightness of the skin along the shaft varies from slightly loose to fairly tight and smooth. Since there is not much loose foreskin left, it is not possible to pull the foreskin to cover over the glans. Sexual pleasure is derived from the exposed glans and exposed inner foreskin along the upper shaft through touch and friction sensation. Instead of deriving sexual pleasure via folding and unfolding the loose foreskin as in the case of the uncircumcised, the inner foreskin (and the glans) can now be directly stimulated, for example, via oral or vaginal contact.

Female Reproductive System

The female reproductive organs can generally be divided into two groups: the internal genitalia and the external genitalia, or vulva. The main internal female sexual organs consist of the ovaries, the fallopian tubes, the uterus, and the vagina. The external genitalia consist of the vaginal opening; inner lips, or labia minora; outer lips, or labia majora; the urethra opening; and the clitoris.

OVARIES

There are two ovaries, each containing many immature eggs, or ova. Normally, during each menstruation cycle, an egg matures and is released into one of the oviducts, or fallopian tubes. The tube then carries the egg downstream toward the uterus. The fallopian tubes also serve as the meeting place for the egg and the sperm from the male.

UTERUS

The uterus, also called the womb, is about the size of a small pear. The fallopian tubes enter the uterus from the top. The lower part of the uterine cavity that forms the narrow base is called the cervical canal.

If the egg is fertilized, it is normally implanted onto the wall of the uterus and grows. For the duration of the pregnancy, it draws its nutrients from the body of the mother. If the egg is not fertilized, then it is discharged during what is called the menstruation period.

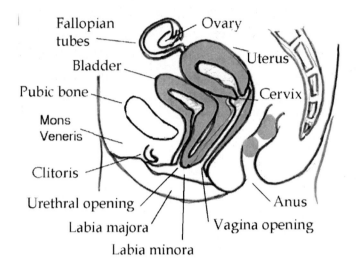

Side view of female reproductive system

The uterus opens into the inner end of the vagina through the uterus neck, or cervix. The cervical passage is very narrow and is framed by strong muscles, to ensure the uterus is virtually germfree.

VAGINA

The vagina is an elastic, muscular canal joining the external vulva (the vagina opening) and the cervix of the uterus. It serves as the receptacle of the male penis during sexual intercourse and as the birth canal during vaginal birth.[49] It consists of three layers of tissues.

The innermost layer (which can be touched through the vaginal opening) consists of mucous membranes and is a surface similar to the lining of the mouth, though softer. It contains folds or wrinkles, which provide sexual pleasure to the male during intercourse. Under sexual arousal, tissue fluids appear on the mucous walls of the vaginal canal as beads, like the moisture droplets formed on an icy-cold glass. This prepares the vagina for easier insertion of the penis.

The second layer is a layer of muscle, concentrated mostly around the outer third of the vagina. At the beginning of arousal, the inner two-thirds of the vagina lengthen and widen, giving the effect of what is called tenting, or ballooning.[50] The purpose of tenting is not altogether clear, although the common speculation is that it allows for accommodating large penis sizes and retention of semen for reproduction. That may partially explain elongation, but what about widening? We will see later that the biblical book of Song of Songs probably describes its purpose during sexual intercourse. As excitement continues, the vagina contracts and grips the penis firmly.[51]

The third layer consists of fibrous tissue that connects to other anatomical structures. An erogenous zone, commonly referred to as the G-spot (also known as the Gräfenberg spot) is said to be located at the anterior wall of the vagina, about two inches (five centimeters) in from the entrance.[52] Some women experience intense pleasure if the G-spot is stimulated appropriately during sexual activity. However, the existence of the G-spot as a distinct structure is still unclear and seems to vary from individual to individual.[53]

VAGINAL OPENING

Near the opening of the vagina, there is normally a thin membrane called the hymen. It has no known physiological function. Once dilated, it never grows back. In some females, the hymen is extremely tough and resistant. In a small number of cases, girls are born without a hymen. There is an opening in the hymen of a virgin of about one inch in diameter. For comfortable intercourse, a diameter of about one and half inches is needed. That is why most brides experience some pain on the first night, although this is usually bearable. To reduce this discomfort so that the penis can enter more comfortably and less painfully for the bride on her first night, she or her bridegroom can perform what is called "vaginal stretching," or "hymen dilation."[54] First, a finger is inserted into the hymen opening. Later two, and optionally three, fingers can be inserted. Pressure is very slowly but firmly exerted down toward her backside, and to the left and right sides. This pressure should be applied for a few minutes and then released. This process is repeated until eventually all the fingers can be inserted fully and comfortably inside the vagina. This process may take fifteen to thirty minutes.

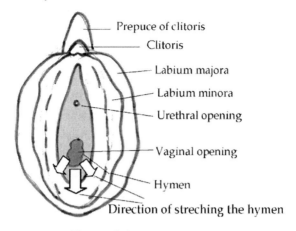

Hymen Dilation

URETHRA

The urethra is the outlet for urination. It is a tube running beneath the pubic bone. Its opening is located between the vaginal opening and the clitoris.

CLITORIS

Located at the top of the vulva region is the mons pubis, which is the pad of fatty tissues covering the pubic bone beneath it. The pair of large "lips," or labia majora, provides a protective cover and conceals the other delicate external organs: the labia minora, clitoris, urethra opening, and vagina opening. The labia minora is a pair of thinner and smaller "lips." Just below it at the upper end is the clitoris, which is the sensitive female organ, similar to the male glans.[55]

It is covered by a layer of skin called the clitoral hood, or prepuce.

The clitoris is the trigger of female desire. Sufficient physical stimulation of the clitoris alone usually produces orgasm in most females. However, direct contact with the clitoris usually produces pain or discomfort instead. Hence, removal of the protective prepuce, such as by circumcision, to expose the clitoris will result in trauma and pain.

At the beginning of arousal, the clitoris may enlarge in some females, while in others the enlargement is not noticeable. Indirect stimulation can be performed by stretching the prepuce and the labia. Direct stimulation should be very gentle, as it is very sensitive and at times should not be touched at all. An alternative is the use of the mouth. As the excitement continues, the clitoris actually is submerged in the engorged surrounding tissues. Because of the ever-changing sensitivity of the clitoris, the wife may want to guide and even take the initiative in the stimulation process.

Mons Veneris

The mons veneris, also known as the mons pubis, is a cushion of body fat above the clitoris covering the pubic bone. It serves as a shock absorber or protective pad. It divides on both sides to form the labia majora.

LABIA MAJORA

The labia majora are also called the outer lips, although they appear more like a mound. They are a pair of parallel folds of flesh, extending on either side of the vulva. They protect and cushion the more delicate external structures of the vulva.

LABIA MINORA

Within the labia majora, is a pair of soft folds of skin called the labia minora, or inner lips. The labia minora connect to the prepuce at the front end and extend on either side of the vaginal opening toward the anus region.

The inner lips are sensitive to touch and give a pleasant sensation. During sexual arousal, the lips expand to two to three times their normal thickness. Since they are connected directly above the clitoris, the tugging and pulling of the lips carries sensation to the clitoris. And since direct stimulation of the clitoris often causes pain or discomfort, manipulation of the inner lips provides a better alternative means of pleasure to the wife.

CHAPTER 6

Physical Intimacy: Oneness

There are three things which are too wonderful for me, yea, four which I know not: The way of an eagle in the air; the way of a serpent upon a rock; the way of a ship in the midst of the sea; and the way of a man with a maiden.
Proverbs 30:18–19

Sexual intimacy in Christian marriage is a learning process. We live in a world brainwashed into believing that it all comes naturally, that we are born with the natural instinct for how to make love, just like the animals around us. However, the primary and only purpose of sexual intercourse for these animals is for reproduction; and by divine design, we are not animals. As we learned earlier, for humans sex is more than just a matter of reproduction.

It is a good sign that today many churches are more open to discussion of the important issues relating to marital intimacy and relationship. There are retreats and camps specifically tailored to counseling and teaching married couples about building genuine intimacy into their relationships. Additional knowledge and skills in regard to intimacy are important, for God has built into our bodies blessings and pleasures for us to enjoy and so that we can appreciate him more.

God designed marriage so that we would not be alone (Genesis 2:18). His design is that husband and wife should be joined into one flesh, not just physically, but also spiritually and psychologically. This oneness does not come naturally, though. We must learn to develop oneness, and this is a lifelong process. A married couple needs to learn how to please each other in their intimate, physical relationship, as well as in the union of spirit, soul, and body. Unfortunately, many publications readily available in bookstores and on the Internet today emphasize lust and self-indulgence rather than the oneness that is the central theme of the love God designed. They acknowledge no distinction between roles for husband and wife and promote sexual practices and acts that are against the teachings of the Bible.

Love Versus Lust

Love and lust have been greatly confused. Lust has been largely substituted for love, especially in relationships between the sexes, but lust is not love. The *Merriam-Webster Dictionary* defines lust as intense or unbridled sexual desire or lasciviousness.[56] The primary difference between love and lust is the attitude of the heart. If you are in love, the attitude of your heart is one of selflessness; the other person is your focus. Lust is self-centered; the focus is on the selfish indulgence of one's own pleasure.

The apostle Paul gives us a list that sums up what love is.

> *Love is always patient; love is always kind; love is never envious or arrogant with pride. Nor is she conceited, and she is never rude; she never thinks just of herself or ever gets annoyed. She never is resentful; is never glad with sin; she's always glad to side with truth, and pleased that truth will win. She bears up under everything; believes the best in all; there is no limit to her hope, and never will she fall. Love never fails.*
> *1 Corinthians 13:4–8 (ISV* [ii]*)*

[ii] We choose the ISV (International Standard Version) here for its vividness and more idiomatic translation over the more literal translation

Perhaps the most familiar verse about love is John 3:16.

For God so loved the world, that he gave his only begotten Son, that whosoever believes in him should not perish, but have everlasting life.
John 3:16

The Greek word for love here is *agape*. This is a sacrificial, impartial, "universal" kind of love, or what we might simply call godly love. Another "type" of love mentioned in the New Testament is *phileo*. *Phileo* love is brotherly love. The apostle Peter, who seemed quite proficient at expressing *phileo* love and was probably very popular because of this, wrote,

Since you have in obedience to the truth purified your souls for a sincere love [phileo] of the brethren, fervently love [agape] one another from the heart.
1 Peter 1:22 (NASB)

Biblical, Christ-like love is the exact opposite of lust, yet the media and entertainment today have blurred the definitions of the two. People are applauded for being free and progressive in their lifestyles, jumping from one bed to another, as if tasting the various fruits. Lust rips the family unit apart, and it is doing so today more than ever.

---

rendered in the King James Version.

The Bible has much to say about lust. Perhaps the first thing that springs to mind is the tenth commandment.

> *You shall not covet your neighbor's house, you shall not covet your neighbor's wife, nor his manservant, nor his maidservant, nor his ox, nor his donkey, nor any thing that is your neighbor's*
> *Exodus 20:17*

The desire to possess someone else's spouse is not only covetousness but also lust.

Another verse that is somewhat controversial but popularly quoted is Mathew 5:28 in Jesus' famous Sermon on the Mount.

> *But I say unto you, That whosoever looks on a woman to lust after her has committed adultery with her already in his heart.*
> *Matthew 5:28*

It is a misconception that looking at women is a sin. If men do not look at women, we have a problem. The key words here are "to lust after," meaning having a desire to have a sexual relationship with her. At some point in time, though, most men will have a desire to marry and have a sexual relationship with a woman. Does that mean we all are committing adultery? Definitely not. That is why it is important not to read verses out of context. The verse immediately before Matthew 5:28 reads:

> *You have heard that it was said by them of old time,*
> *You shall not commit adultery.*
> *Matthew 5:27*

Clearly Jesus was on the topic of adultery, as defined in the Ten Commandments; that is, as having a sexual relationship with someone other than one's own spouse. With this background knowledge, verse 28 obviously refers to someone burning with lust to commit adultery (and thus searching for targets), and Jesus says such a person has already committed the sin even before the actual act. Proverbs has a similar verse.

> *Lust not after her beauty in your heart; neither let her allure you with her eyelids.*
> *Proverbs 6:25*

Again, we should be careful not to take this out of context. Verse 29 provides further information about the woman mentioned here.

> *So is he that goes in to his neighbor's wife; whosoever touches her shall not be innocent.*
> *Proverbs 6:29*

She is someone else's wife! God creates women with beauty to be admired, and admiring women is not a sin, except when one lusts for adultery. James, the brother of Jesus, sums up most succinctly the process whereby lust tempts and lures us into sin.

> *Let no man say when he is tempted, I am tempted of God: for God cannot be tempted with evil, neither tempts he any man: But every man is tempted, when he is drawn away of his own lust, and enticed. Then when lust has conceived, it brings forth sin: and sin, when it is finished, brings forth death.*
> James 1:13–15

Sexual Temptations

In our world today we are constantly being bombarded with all sorts of sexual temptations through magazines, newspapers, TV, advertisements, the Internet, movies, billboards, pornography, jokes, and on and on. Even children's materials sometimes have inappropriate content. Growing up under such influences, many become accustomed to them and just take them as the norm. As a result, many indulge in sexual sin, and many even become addicted to it.

It's very unfortunate when a person's career is ruined due to a sexual scandal or when someone dies due to a sexually transmitted disease or when a family breaks up due to infidelity. Even Christians are not immune. Sexual sins not only damage the ones who commit them but also inflict pain and suffering on the people around them.

I recently visited Shanghai. In the West, we have contraceptives offered in vending machines located in some convenient locations, such as in restrooms. China has these products, with erotic descriptions, prominently displayed for sale in the hotel rooms for "your convenience."

How can we keep ourselves pure and away from these temptations? There are many suggestions. Some advocate leading a life in isolation from these temptations. They suggest getting rid of all those things that lead to temptation—no TV, no newspapers, no magazines, no Internet, no living in the cities or around people who are living an impure lifestyle, and no telephones because we may be tempted to dial those special numbers. So there are people who live in caves or mountain hideouts so they can meditate and not be tempted. There are also people who live in villages where they congregate with only the like-minded. Communication with the outside world is discouraged. They often quote Bible verses to support their arguments, verses such as 1 Corinthians 6:18; 10:14; 1 Timothy 6:11; 2 Timothy 2:22; or the Lord's Prayer, which speaks about avoiding temptation.

> *And lead us not into temptation, but deliver us from evil.*
> *Matthew 6:13*

Many view the struggle with sexual temptation as simply a matter of controlling sexual thoughts and feelings. The victory comes when they can exercise control over their wandering minds and thus avoid the opportunities for lust.

Meditation and thought control have been suggested. And, indeed, praying to God, asking for help in cleansing our lustful thoughts, and pursuing self-control should come naturally to any Christian facing temptations. Often quoted is Paul's advice on sinful thoughts.

> *Casting down arguments, and every high thing that exalts itself against the knowledge of God, and bringing into captivity every thought to the obedience of Christ.*
> *2 Corinthians 10:5*

Some believe sexual temptation is an addiction or compulsion and hence recommend adopting an approach often applied to alcoholism.[57] This approach, known as the AA (Alcoholics Anonymous) program, sees alcoholism as a symptom of deeper hurt. The idea is that alcoholism is a progressive illness that cannot be cured in the ordinary sense of the term; however, it can be arrested through total abstinence from alcohol in any form.[58] The focal point is the alcoholic rather than alcoholism. The cure is to admit the addiction, turn one's life over to the care of a Higher Power, and take steps to mend relationships with those one has harmed. Once denial is removed, then the feeling of inadequacy can be eliminated and the real roots of the problem—loneliness, insecurity, trauma, etc.—can be healed and the addiction controlled. It is not surprising that many similar groups have sprung up in response to various other disorders, such as Narcotics Anonymous, Gamblers Anonymous, Sex and Love Addicts Anonymous,

Sexual Compulsives Anonymous, Sex Addicts Anonymous, and Sexaholics Anonymous.[59] Are these recovery programs effective? In some cases they appear to be, and AA at least is comparable to other forms of therapy;[60] but there are many criticisms.[61]

God wants us to lead a life free from sexual sin and addictions. There are a number of reasons for this. First, engaging in sexual activities outside marriage violates God's law and is a sin. The seventh commandment states:

> *You shall not commit adultery.*
> *Exodus 20:14*

Indulgence in these activities will lead to committing other sins, for example, breaking the tenth commandment.

> *You shall not covet your neighbor's wife.*
> *Exodus 20:17*

Second, extramarital sexual activities usually lead to divorce and other complications, such as child custody disputes, stress, and depression.

Living in solitude is not an option, for this stands in direct contradiction to the example Jesus set down for us. We see Jesus eating with "sinners" and mixing with tax collectors, the Samaritans, and other outcasts of society. He wanted to bring these people into the kingdom of God, to save them from their sins. Thus, on the one hand, we are to lead holy lives. On the other hand, we are to live within the community, facing temptations daily and yet without being overcome by them.

The apostle Paul told the Corinthians to stay clear of sexual immorality and advised them to each have his or her own spouse so that they not fall prey to temptations.

> *Nevertheless, to avoid fornication, let every man have his own wife, and let every woman have her own husband.*
> 1 Corinthians 7:2

In those days, Corinth was a great city. It was a prosperous and wealthy hub of commerce, lying on natural trade routes connecting Greece with the rest of the world. Corinth also was an important religious center for the Greeks because the temple dedicated to Aphrodite, the Greek goddess of love, was located there.[62] It is said that at one time a thousand "sacred" priestesses were engaged in cultic sexual activities there as part of fertility rituals.[63] It was precisely these practices that Paul addressed in the letter to the Corinthian church as he urged his readers to exercise self-control and avoid participation in these rites. Yet to a city with such abominations, the apostle Paul brought the gospel of Jesus Christ, and the gospel thrived there. The Corinthian church continued to struggle for a long time with these moral issues. But Paul clearly and forcefully laid down the basic principles that sex outside marriage is immoral and forbidden and that husband and wife have moral obligations to help each other to overcome sexual temptations.

> *Let the husband render unto the wife her due: and likewise also the wife unto the husband. The wife has not power over her own body, but the husband: and likewise also the husband has not power over his own body, but the wife. Deprive not one the other, except it be with consent for a time, that you may give yourselves to fasting and prayer; and come together again, that Satan tempt you not for your lack of self-control.*
> *1 Corinthians 7:3–5*

It is easy to misconstrue Paul's message of equality here to mean there are no differences between the sexes. If that were the case, though, it would conflict with Paul's letter to the Ephesians, as we discussed in chapter 3. We must understand that while the husband and wife are equally responsible for the well-being of the family, in love the husband is the head and the wife is the body.

Let us recap Paul's exact intention in what he wrote concerning the sexes in his first letter to the Corinthians.

> *Now concerning the things of which you wrote unto me: It is good for a man not to touch a woman.*
> *1 Corinthians 7:1*

Clearly, this refers to those like Paul himself who have decided to remain single and celibate. The apostle then goes on to explain cases where one cannot withstand the temptations.

> *Nevertheless, to avoid fornication, let every man have his own wife, and let every woman have her own husband. Let the husband render unto the wife her due: and likewise also the wife unto the husband. The wife has not power over her own body, but the husband: and likewise also the husband has not power over his own body, but the wife. Deprive not one the other, except it be with consent for a time, that you may give yourselves to fasting and prayer; and come together again, that Satan tempt you not for your lack of self-control.*
> 1 Corinthians 7:2–5

Paul is saying, "Get married to avoid fornication!" In Ephesians he was explaining the beauty of sex in bonding the husband and wife and allowing them to know God's love in a deeper way. Sex is holy and sanctioned by God. In 1 Corinthians, however, Paul indicates that sex within marriage is an appropriate weapon against sexual temptations. Thus, he commands us to take care of the sexual needs of our spouses. It is our duty to our spouse to ensure his or her sexual urges are satisfied and sexual tensions are released, for this guards against adultery.

Phases of the Sexual Response Cycle

Apart from extramarital sexual temptations and within the intimacy of their marriage, a man and a woman gradually learn the meaning of the one-flesh relationship (or oneness) God designed, as they express their love to each other. This oneness is not limited to the physical but also encompasses other aspects of life, such as the emotional, the spiritual, the mind, and the soul. The physical aspect, however, is usually the starting point of the oneness. Hence, learning the physiological phases of sexual response helps to enhance the physical intimacy and bond building. It also helps us to better understand the lyrics in the Song of Songs, a book in the Bible that describes how a married couple engage in lovemaking. That book is the subject of our study in the next chapter.

It is well established that physiological responses during sexual activities generally can be divided into a number of phases for both male and female. The Masters-and-Johnson model divides the phases into four: excitement, plateau, orgasm, and resolution. [64] The Helen Singer Kaplan model has three phases: desire, excitement, and orgasm.[65] Helen Singer Kaplan considers Masters and Johnson's excitement and plateau phases as a continuous phase in which the arousal increases over time. She believes that without desire, we are not going to get excited about sex. The phases listed below represent an adaptation of the two models.

DESIRE

Desire is the appetite, drive, or libido that originates from the brain. Both lust and love can produce such brain activities. Lust is self-centered and indulges in self-gratification, whereas love focuses on the spouse and derives satisfaction and excitement from pleasing the spouse. The Song of Songs clearly displays the couple admiring each other with the sense of belonging. The desire to please is explicitly demonstrated.

Often desire is displayed days before the intimacy even begins. The thoughtfulness, the longing to be together, and the desire to see each other are all part of this leading phase that enhances the intimacy. Often this desire dwindles after marriage. Therefore, it is important to make an effort to maintain the desire of one another. The sexual roles of husband and wife as designed by God are the recipe to keep the desire burning. The true nature and meaning of sex can be understood only when the two express their love in accord with the love between Jesus and his church. Our desire first should be toward Jesus. Then the desire toward our spouse will burn even more strongly.

AROUSAL

In the arousal phase, commonly known as foreplay, pleasure is derived from the senses in the body, particularly from the genitals. Stimulating these senses sends a delightful sensation to the brain and causes reflex vasodilation, or widening, of genital blood vessels and thus increased blood flow. The first sign of arousal in the husband is the erection of the penis. Very quickly he may be ready to enter the next phase, if continuously stimulated. It is necessary to prolong his stay in the arousal phase, as the wife is not ready yet. She is just starting to feel aroused, and lubrication of the vagina is just beginning. The inner two-thirds of the vagina begin to expand and balloon in what is generally referred to as tenting. At this stage, insertion of the penis does not give much sensation to her, and there is no gripping sensation for the husband either.

The husband needs to put more effort into the foreplay at this point. Foreplay is a very important part of expressing love. It includes, but is not limited to, kissing, embracing, petting, fondling, and caressing. Torso-to-torso rubbing, thigh-to-thigh moving, and stroking should be part of the experience. We will see these movements in the Song of Songs. The foreplay should be a very relaxed experience. It takes time to fully enjoy each other, and it should be a whole-body experience. The wife will be ready only near the end of the next phase, the plateau phase. So there is still a long way to go. Hasty passage into the next phase can push the relationship further apart and reduce the interest in intimacy.

It is necessary to prolong this phase for ten to fifteen minutes or more in order to get the wife ready. During this phase, erections may wax and wane. To keep the erection full, and hence the desire going, the wife may need to occasionally fondle the shaft and the glans of the penis. The buildup of pleasure should be slow and leisurely. If the husband is circumcised, fondling the glans can be very painful. In this modern age, suitable lubricants are readily available. In ancient times, the only remedy was to perform oral sex. In some more conservative Christian circles, it is assumed that the Bible prohibits oral sex since there do not seem to be any biblical references to it. This is actually incorrect. We will demonstrate that, in fact, the Bible has devoted the whole book of the Song of Songs to describing intimate sexual activities, including this one.

PLATEAU

A gradual transition into the plateau phase helps to enhance the intimacy. The transition is not well defined, though.

Prolonging the plateau phase intensifies the ultimate orgasm of both spouses. The Song describes some of these activities and how the husband can bring the wife to a high level of excitement and how the wife can help the husband to continue his zeal to accomplish his goal. His goal is to please her and to bring her to orgasm. Her goal is to prolong this phase so that he can achieve his goal of pleasuring her. It is in this phase that the wife should learn how to submit herself to him. Learning to submit takes lots of willpower, trust in her husband, and understanding of his physiological responses. The husband needs to learn how to make sacrifices for her by controlling himself so that he does not reach ejaculation. Learning this takes time, effort, perseverance, and an awareness of his own physiological states of excitement.

In this phase the bodily changes are more prominent. The nipples of the wife become firmer. As the excitement increases, the nipples become less prominent because of the engorgement of the surrounding breasts. The wife is more receptive to fondling of the genitals, although gentleness is still the key word. She tends to be able to sustain the level of excitement and to gradually increase it. However, the husband tends to get excited easily, but after a while the excitement tends to wane. As in the arousal phase, the wife may fondle his glans, shaft, and testicles to maintain his level of excitement. However, she must beware of exciting him too much or it may trigger ejaculation. His testicles enlarge by about 50 percent and pull more closely to the body.

The wife's clitoris becomes engorged, and the inner lips thicken to about two to three times their normal size. As the excitement continues, the outer third of the vagina reduces to as much as half its original diameter. At this stage, the vagina is ready to grip the penis. The inner lips also turn from pinkish-red to a brighter red, or purple. The pulse rate increases, and there is a general flush of skin.

Communication with each other regarding the level of excitement is important. This helps each one to be better prepared in his or her role. One method to achieve this is for the husband and wife to take turns giving stimulation to the other. When the husband focuses on giving stimulation, the wife stays back and enjoys the pleasure. It is then the wife's turn to provide the stimulation. For prolonging the love play, the wife should stop stimulating two to three seconds before the husband feels the onset of orgasm.

ORGASM AND EJACULATION

Orgasm and ejaculation is commonly thought to be the next phase. However, the Song of Songs seems to indicate that these are separate events, even though male orgasm usually is closely followed by ejaculation. Dictionary definitions often blend the two together, as if they are one and the same thing. There are many discussions on this topic; however, the sciences are still very primitive. For our purpose, we will loosely define the term *ejaculation* as the emission and ejection of seminal fluid from the body.

We will treat *orgasm* as a psychological, highly pleasurable experience marked by peaks of emotional, physical, and psychological sexual pleasure. It is the beginning phase of the pleasurable feeling that is still controllable.

In the Song of Songs, male orgasm is interspersed at several points along the plateau phase. The husband can move very quickly from arousal, through plateau, and ejaculation in a very short time if he is excited too quickly. On the other hand, he can prolong his stay in the plateau phase without ejaculation. To achieve this, the wife should focus on the inner thighs, testicles, the shaft, and the glans, starting gently in the arousal phase and gradually increasing the duration and firmness of the caressing in the plateau phase. The aim is to sustain him at a high level of excitement but without triggering ejaculation.

We still do not know much about female orgasm. To evolutionary biologists, the male orgasmic function makes perfect sense. They argue that it ensures the survival of the human race by offering a physiological motivation to pursue and inseminate females. They claim that the speed and consistency with which heterosexual men achieve orgasm via vaginal intercourse also supports its classification as a beneficial adaptation. However, there is not yet any convincing explanation as to why women also need orgasm and why there is the disparity between male and female orgasmic functions. Many theories have been put forward, but female orgasm has remained an "evolutionary mystery."[66] All the propositions and explanations have been challenged, and there are clear evidences that contradict these evolutionary propositions.[67,] Zoologist Robin Baker popularized the theory of "sperm wars," whereby orgasm is said to endow women with a reproductive advantage in retaining sperm and thus increasing their fertility. However, the thesis does not stand up to further scrutiny.[68]

Observing the disparity between male and female rates of orgasm and the various "scientific explanations" given for female sexual functions and orgasm, Elisabeth A. Lloyd explores the persistent mystery as to why women evolved to have orgasms while most of man's primate relatives didn't. [69] She disagrees with the evolutionary arguments, ranging from pair bonding (orgasms make females more likely to form stable partnerships) to sperm competition (orgasms expel previously deposited sperm from other sexual partners), and believes they represent a history of missteps, misuse of evidence, and missed references. She dismisses adaptation theory by demonstrating how most of the evolutionary accounts either are in conflict with, or lack, certain types of evidence necessary to make their cases. The conclusion, Lloyd argues, must surely be that the female orgasm has no biological function and does not serve an evolutionary purpose. Females do not need orgasm to reproduce. All the conflicting "scientific" explanations suggest that we should be very careful about accepting any of them as truth. Indeed, we should look at the Bible for clues and answers, for female orgasm is by divine design and in that design serves a purpose.

The common perception that a couple ideally should aim at achieving orgasm simultaneously is not what is described in the Song of Songs. In the Song, the couple alternate caressing each other while the receiving spouse lies back and enjoys the intimacy and delight. The wife may reach orgasm as she wishes, without any restriction. However, the husband avoids ejaculation as he approaches orgasm. The reason for this sacrifice originates in the ancient Mosaic laws.

These laws of love, intimacy, and hygiene are found in Leviticus 15, which deals specifically with normal and abnormal secretions from the male and the female organs.[70] They are commonly referred to as "uncleanness of secretions," or "personal impurities."

The issue of cleanness and uncleanness relates to the worship life of the covenant community, as carried out by the priests and their assistants who served in the temple. When a person was unclean, he or she was disqualified from participation in the worship. "Unclean" thus did not mean "dirty." It merely identified a person as unsuitable to perform any holy duties in the temple.

In Leviticus 15 there are five cases relating to "uncleanness."

Male having abnormal discharge from the organ (verses 2–15)

Male having emission of semen (verses 16–18)

Female having abnormal discharge from the organ (verses 25–30)

Female having her normal monthly period (verses 19–24)

Male and female having sexual intercourse and there is an emission of semen from the male (verse 18)

It is not clear what the abnormal discharges are, but from the remedies described in the passage, we can deduce that these relate to sexual diseases and infections. We also can deduce that there are two types of "uncleanness": the abnormal discharges and the normal discharges. The abnormal discharges required a sin offering and burnt offering, and the person had to follow certain procedures before he or she could be declared clean.

> *And on the eighth day he shall take for him two turtledoves, or two young pigeons, and come before the LORD unto the door of the tabernacle of meeting, and give them unto the priest: And the priest shall offer them, the one for a sin offering, and the other for a burnt offering; and the priest shall make an atonement for him before the LORD for his discharge. . . . And on the eighth day she shall take unto her two turtledoves, or two young pigeons, and bring them unto the priest, to the door of the tabernacle of meeting. And the priest shall offer the one for a sin offering, and the other for a burnt offering; and the priest shall make an atonement for her before the LORD for the discharge of her uncleanness.*
> *Leviticus 15:14-15, 29–30*

In the case of a woman having her normal period, the law clearly was designed to protect her against any sexual activities that may cause infections during the normal waiting period of seven days. During those ancient days three thousand years ago, hygiene was constantly a problem. Note that there was no sin or burnt offering required because this was a normal discharge.

For the same reason, there also was no sin or burnt offering for ejaculation of the male. However, the treatment of the uncleanness due to ejaculation was quite different. Two different situations are described here. One applied to the man, and the other to the woman.

> *And if any man's semen go out from him, then he shall wash all his flesh in water, and be unclean until the evening. And every garment, and every skin, on which is the semen, shall be washed with water, and be unclean until the evening. The woman also with whom man shall lie and have an emission of semen, they shall both bathe themselves in water, and be unclean until the eveni*
> *Leviticus 15:16-18*

The popular interpretations and biblical commentaries hold the view that the seminal emission in verse 16 relates to involuntary, nocturnal emission.[71] Deuteronomy 23 often is quoted in support of this.[72]

> *If there be among you any man, that is unclean by reason of some occurrence in the night, then shall he go outside the camp, he shall not come inside the camp: But it shall be, when evening comes on, he shall wash himself with water: and when the sun is down, he shall come into the camp again. You shall have a place also outside the camp, where you shall go out.*
> *Deuteronomy 23:10–12*

What we often overlook is that Moses' address to the nation of Israel recorded in the book of Deuteronomy was given on the plain of Moab just prior to their entrance into the Promised Land of Canaan and was meant to prepare the nation for wars ahead. Deuteronomy restates the laws in Exodus, Leviticus, and Numbers.

The book of Leviticus serves a different purpose. The name of the book comes from *Levi,* one of the twelve tribes of Israel. The tribe of Levi was chosen by God to be priests and assistants in the service of the tabernacle for life. Leviticus covers national and personal laws concerning worship and serving in various religious activities. As one would expect, God demanded the highest standards in all respects from people who wanted to participate in these ceremonies.

The nocturnal emission in Deuteronomy specifically required that the man not only wash himself but also go outside the camp for the whole day till evening. However, as the laws in Leviticus were for worship and devotion to God, we would expect the treatment of seminal emissions to cover all possible cases of seminal emissions. We can see that the wording of Leviticus 15:16 is indeed very general and all-inclusive:

And if any man's semen go out from him . . .
Leviticus 15:16

It does not say "at night," or "nocturnal," or "naturally," or "involuntarily." Thus, the verse could include various cases when the man has his seminal emission go "out from him," such as in masturbation, nocturnal emissions, and sexual activities between the husband and wife (both with and without sexual intercourse). The man is unclean because his semen has gone out of his body (verse 16). Anything (garment, his skin, etc.) that comes into contact with his semen is also considered unclean (verse 17).

Leviticus 15:18 deals with the case of the woman. Two things must happen for this law to apply to her: There must be sexual intercourse, and there must be seminal emission. In the Bible, it is common to refer to "a man lying with a woman," referring to having sexual intercourse with her. If a man has sexual intercourse with a woman and ejaculates, then he is considered unclean under Leviticus 15:16, and she is also unclean under Leviticus 15:18. Note the conjunction "also" in verse 18, which indicates the condition of the woman is related to the man, or is a continuation of the line of reasoning in verses 16–17. In particular, verse 17 implies that anything that comes into contact with the semen is also considered unclean. It must be washed in water and is unclean until the evening. It is common knowledge that after sexual intercourse, some semen in the woman will eventually flow out of her body. Thus, she has the semen gone out from her, and her skin comes into contact with it. Verse 18 indicates that in such a case, she *also* is considered unclean. From these verses, it is reasonable to argue that any person or things that comes into contact with the semen is considered unclean. Again, as explained earlier, this does not mean they are "dirty," as in our modern usage of the word.

What happens when there is sexual intercourse but there is no seminal emission? Of course, the law does not apply. In fact, we can also deduce that as long as there is no seminal emission, then these laws do not apply to either sex.

If there is seminal emission, the sexual activities come to a halt for the rest of the day. The laws do not mention anything about the female ejaculation, or orgasm. Thus, the laws seem to encourage the male to exercise self-control by prolonging ejaculation while there is no such restriction on the female.

RESOLUTION

Relaxation, or the resolution phase, is the refractory period immediately following ejaculation. During this time a male is unable to achieve another erection or orgasm. He feels a deep and often pleasurable sense of relaxation, enhanced intimacy, and often fatigue, or sleepiness. Women experience a similar resolution period, but usually the recovery time is much shorter. Some women are capable of a rapid return to the orgasm phase if further sexual stimulation is applied.

Even though love play is over, it is important that husband and wife continue their love affections with tender hugs and kisses. With these activities the transition from excitement to normal level will be smooth and less abrupt, providing a more romantic ending to the whole love play.

Effects of Circumcision

We have described the physiological phases of sexual responses without much consideration of the effects of circumcision. We have already discussed circumcision at some length and described the difference between the *periah* type of circumcision practiced today and Abrahamic, or *milah*, circumcision. Here we will focus briefly on circumcision as it relates to sexual intimacy.

Abrahamic circumcision removes only the excess foreskin so that a flaccid penis will have the glans either fully covered or mostly covered by the foreskin. When erect, the glans is fully exposed. Instead of having the loose, inner foreskin still folded over the glans, now the inner foreskin lies along the upper part of the shaft.

During sexual intercourse between an uncircumcised husband and his wife, the male foreskin, being fairly long, serves as a double-layered conduit in which the penis glides. The muscles at the opening of the vagina grasp hold of the loose foreskin of the penis so that on the outward glide, the grasp forces the foreskin to fold and cover the glans penis. On the inward glide, the foreskin unfolds. However, because of the excess, the foreskin provides a smooth conduit for the shaft to glide in. The penis does not provide much arousal to the female while gliding in and out inside its own foreskin. The clitoris remains as if in the far distance, seemingly detached and disengaged from all the action happening an inch away.

Most females need clitoral stimulation to experience orgasm,[73] and normally they don't get it during intercourse because the clitoris is located outside the vagina and a few inches above it at the top end of the vaginal lips. Sexual intercourse simply does not provide enough clitoral stimulation to allow them to reach orgasm. It is not surprising that many surveys show that only 20 to 30 percent of females attain orgasm during sexual intercourse.[74]

In the case of a circumcised man, the glans of the penis, as well as the inner foreskin, will come into direct contact with the vagina during intercourse. When fully aroused (close to the end of the plateau phase), the outer third of the vagina contracts and firmly grips the penis. Since there is no loose foreskin, during the inward stroke of the penis, the vagina opening, together with the labia minora, are dragged along. This in turn causes the prepuce to be pulled downward. During the outward stroke, the labia minora return to their original position, which in turn causes the prepuce to flex back. The movements of the prepuce cause pleasurable feelings in the clitoris. Thus, in general, the wives of circumcised males are more likely to attain sexual satisfaction during intercourse.

In the next chapter, we will reveal more secrets that will help to increase the woman's pleasurable experience. For now, we can see the advantage of circumcision over uncircumcision. Indeed, the apostle Paul says that circumcision does benefit. However, there are certain conditions.

> *For circumcision verily profits, if you keep the law: but if you are a breaker of the law, your circumcision is made uncircumcision.*
> *Romans 2:25*

> *Therefore if the uncircumcision keeps the righteousness of the law, shall not his uncircumcision be counted for circumcision? And*

shall not uncircumcision which is by nature, if it fulfills the law, judge you, who by the letter and circumcision do transgress the law?
Romans 2:26–27

We have seen many arguments about circumcision focusing on the second and third of the above verses while ignoring the first. Clearly, the last two verses are the preconditions to circumcision. We totally miss Paul's argument if we say that Paul abolishes circumcision or discourages circumcision. Paul is saying that circumcision of the *heart* (keeping the laws) is more important than physical circumcision. However, if a person does have a circumcised heart (i.e., has love), then his physical circumcision will benefit him (and her) further. Again, in 1 Corinthians Paul emphasizes the importance of circumcision of the heart by rewording it as keeping God's commandments.

Circumcision is nothing, and uncircumcision is nothing, but the keeping of the commandments of God.
1 Corinthians 7:19

Caring for his wife as if she were his own body is a clear expression of a husband's obedience to God's love commands and an indication of a *circumcised heart*.

So ought men to love their wives as their own bodies. He that loves his wife loves himself. For no

> man ever yet hated his own flesh; but nourishes and cherishes it, even as the Lord the church. Ephesians 5:28–29

Circumcision of the Heart and Emotions

To love God means to meticulously submit to him of our own accord in order to please him. Loving God requires us to cultivate the spiritual relationship with God with all our heart, and with all our soul, and with all our might (Deuteronomy 6:5). Loving God means constantly longing for communion with him; it means feeling happy and joyful when with him but unhappy and miserable when without him.[75] In other words, we think of him and long for him. We are emotionally attached to him. In light of this, Jesus' figure of the vine and the branches takes on a whole new dimension and meaning.

> *I am the vine, you are the branches: He that abides in me, and I in him, the same brings forth much fruit: for without me you can do nothing. John 15:5*

Christians are attached to Jesus, not only spiritually but also emotionally. Spiritual attachment comes from the reestablishment of our spiritual relationship with God when we receive Jesus as our Savior. We draw our spiritual nourishment from Jesus, for he is the source of our spiritual needs. Through him, we grow spiritually and bear spiritual fruit.

> *But the fruit of the Spirit is love, joy, peace, longsuffering, gentleness, goodness, faith, meekness, self-control: against such there is no law.*
>
> Galatians 5:22–23

We also draw our emotions from him, for his thoughts become our thoughts, his purpose becomes our purpose, his commandments become our commandments, his love for the world becomes our love, and his holiness becomes our holiness. Through our attachment to God, our emotional needs are fully met. Our feelings of hunger for God's Word, courage to do his works, calmness, wisdom, self-esteem, sense of belonging, perseverance, and peace all come from him.

The heart is seen as the source of all these spiritual and emotional feelings and needs.[76] Jesus says,

> *If a man loves me, he will keep my words: and my Father will love him, and we will come unto him, and make our abode with him.*
> John 14:23

Paul says that Jesus actually dwells in our heart.

> *Christ may dwell in your hearts by faith.*
> Ephesians 3:17

Hence, we are the temple of God.

> *Know you not that you are the temple of God, and that the Spirit of God dwells in you?*
> *1 Corinthians 3:16*

The temple in Jerusalem was a place of worship. God's law (the ark of the covenant containing the Ten Commandments) was placed within the most holy place of the temple (the very heart). This was a most sacred place and was called the Holy of Holies. The Holy of Holies was separated from the rest of the Holy Place by a thick veil, or curtain. When people worshiped God, they looked to the place where his law was kept and sought to keep the law by obeying it.

Today the temple of God is no longer located in Jerusalem. It now resides in each and every Christian. It is in our hearts. We have to keep it sacred and holy and worship God in spirit and in truth.

> *God is a Spirit: and they that worship him must worship him in spirit and in truth.*
> *John 4:24*

Some interpret "in spirit and in truth" as worshiping God from our heart (in spirit) and in harmony with his Word (in truth). Note, however, that Jesus begins by saying that God is a spirit. Thus, worshiping God in spirit and in truth refers to "the offering of the soul rather than the formal offering of the body—the homage of the heart rather than that of the lips."[77] In the Old Testament, many elements of worship were a shadow of what was to come. For example, the continual sacrifice of goats and calves symbolized and anticipated the once-and-for-all sacrifice of Jesus.

> *Neither by the blood of goats and calves, but by his own blood he entered in once into the holy place, having obtained eternal redemption for us.*
> *Hebrews 9:12*

The emphasis is on what is true (real), not on the symbols. When Jesus died on the cross, the veil in the temple was torn from top to bottom, signifying that from that point on, people could worship God directly.

> *Jesus, when he had cried again with a loud voice, yielded up his spirit. And, behold, the veil of the temple was torn in two from the top to the bottom.*
> *Matthew 27:50–51*

To worship means to express reverence, honor, and intense love for God and to submit to him and fulfill his commandments. True acts of worship are not external rituals that draw attention to ourselves; rather, they are acts of submission with our whole heart, body, mind, soul, and spirit made possible through the Holy Spirit.

> *I beseech you therefore, brethren, by the mercies of God, that you present your bodies a living sacrifice, holy, acceptable [pleasing] unto God, which is your reasonable service.*
> *Romans 12:1*

However, our hearts still can be veiled and dull.

> *But their minds were blinded: for until this day remains the same veil not taken away in the reading of the old covenant; which veil is done away in Christ. But even unto this day, when Moses is read, the veil is upon their hearts.*
> *2 Corinthians 3:14–15*

The people Moses led through the wilderness were a flock of stubborn and stiff-necked people. Their hearts were veiled. That is, they had turned away from God; they were separated from him and were not looking at God. That was why Moses wanted them to be circumcised in their hearts. He wanted them to come closer to God and have their hearts filled with the love of God and a submissive attitude toward him.

> *And the LORD your God will circumcise your heart, and the heart of your descendants, to love the LORD your God with all your heart, and with all your soul, that you may live.*
> *Deuteronomy 30:6*

The removal of filthiness, lust, indulgence, and other sins was not the original intent of circumcision. Circumcision is all about love. Circumcision of the heart is about spiritual love—the love that led Jesus to die for us and to put the Holy Spirit in our hearts when we receive Jesus as our Savior.

In Deuteronomy 10:16, Moses commanded his people,

> *Circumcise therefore the foreskin of your heart, and be no more stiff-necked.*
> *Deuteronomy 10:16*

The word *therefore* indicates that the reasons for circumcision of the heart precede this verse. What are they?

> *And now, Israel, what does the LORD your God require of you, but to fear the LORD your God, to walk in all his ways, and to love him, and to serve the LORD your God with all your heart and with all your soul, To keep the commandments of the LORD, and his statutes, which I command you this day for your good? Behold, the heaven and the heaven of heavens is the LORD'S your God, the earth also, with all that is in it. Only the LORD had a delight in your fathers to love them, and he chose their descendants after them, even you above all people, as it is this day.*
> *Deuteronomy 10:12–15*

Again, we can summarize all the reasons in one word: love. Circumcision of the heart is about love. It is not about purification, as we often hear. The "foreskin" is not viewed as something dirty or filthy that must be put aside.

> *Behold, the days come, says the LORD, that I will punish all them who are circumcised with the uncircumcised; Egypt, and Judah, and Edom, and*

> *the children of Ammon, and Moab, and all that are in the farthest corners, that dwell in the wilderness: for all these nations are uncircumcised, and all the house of Israel are uncircumcised in the heart.*
> *Jeremiah 9:25–26*

"Uncircumcised in the heart" simply means Israel did not love God. Because of that, God was treating them as if they had never been circumcised in the flesh, meaning they were just like those nations around them.

Love from the heart is more important than the physical symbol of circumcision.

> *For he is not a Jew, who is one outwardly; neither is that circumcision, which is outward in the flesh: But he is a Jew, who is one inwardly; and circumcision is that of the heart, in the spirit, and not in the letter; whose praise is not of men, but of God.*
> *Romans 2:28–29*

Unlike the circumcision in the flesh, which is performed by the hand of man, the circumcision of the heart is performed by God himself (Deuteronomy 30:6). This is done when Jesus removes our sins so that we are reconciled to God and the Holy Spirit resides in us.

> *For in him dwells all the fullness of the Deity bodily. And you are complete in him, who is the head of all principality and power: In whom also you are*

> *circumcised with the circumcision made without hands, in putting off the body of the sins of the flesh by the circumcision of Christ.*
> *Colossians 2:9–11*

The sins of the flesh mentioned here are not sins coming from the foreskin. "Flesh" is often mistakenly referred to as the foreskin. Instead, it refers to sexual sins such as lust, adultery, fornication, and incest.

Abraham was considered a righteous man before he received the divine command of circumcision, not after.

> *And he received the sign of circumcision, a seal of the righteousness of the faith which he had yet being uncircumcised.*
> *Romans 4:11*

In a similar manner, we can be circumcised in the heart only after we are declared righteous in the eyes of God through the putting away of our sins by Jesus.

Both circumcision in the flesh (foreskin) and the circumcision of the heart relate to love. This love originates from God and is manifested in Jesus Christ, who sacrificed his life on the cross so that we could be reconciled to God and have eternal and abundant life. The physical circumcision unveils the intimate part in the sexual relationship in marriage. The circumcision of the heart unveils the innermost self (which has been made righteous by Jesus through his blood) in our spiritual, intimate relationship with

God. Because of this righteousness in the eyes of God, we are able to love him, serve him, and please him. Husbands also are able to love their wives, treat them with dignity and pride, and lead in the sexual relationship as God commands. Perhaps we can conclude that circumcision acts like a "bridge" as it connects the divine love (circumcision of the heart) and the earthly love (the physical circumcision). We cannot fully enjoy the oneness of marriage that is expressed in physical intimacy unless we have experienced an intimate, spiritual relationship of love with our heavenly Father.

Summary

God designed marriage to be a one-flesh relationship. Sexual intimacy is a key part of this relationship. As such, it is important that husband and wife learn to please one another in this aspect of marriage.

We are bombarded daily by sexual temptations that appeal to lust and are based on the idea that we should seek to please ourselves. It is crucial that we distinguish between biblical love and the lust that characterizes the world we live in. Genuine, Christ-like love is always focused on the other person. It is not selfish or self-seeking. As we follow this model of love, we will obey God's commands and find sexual fulfillment in marriage. Such fulfillment is a powerful safeguard against the temptations that confront us.

A man and woman gradually learn the meaning of the oneness God designed as they express their love to each other. Learning the physiological phases of sexual response helps the couple to grow in their relationship and enjoy the physical bond. As that bond grows, so do the psychological and spiritual bonds between them. It is important to remember, however, that physical intimacy in marriage, while a key to marital satisfaction, can never be completely satisfying unless there is a growing, dynamic relationship with God that is characterized by a love that is expressed in our desire to serve and please him.

CHAPTER 7

Physical Intimacy: A Biblical Picture

I am the rose of Sharon, and the lily of the valleys. As the lily among thorns, so is my love among the daughters. As the apple tree among the trees of the wood, so is my beloved among the sons. I sat down under his shadow with great delight, and his fruit was sweet to my taste.
Song of Songs 2:1–3

Since physical, or sexual, intimacy is such an important part of marriage, it is not surprising that an entire book of the Bible is dedicated to this theme. The Song of Songs, or the Song of Solomon, is one of the shortest books in the Bible, containing only 117 verses. Despite this, it contains a wealth of truth and knowledge. It is commonly recognized that the book is a love story between a husband and wife, from courtship to consummation. However, there are many interpretations of what this "love story" is really about, with many interpreters seeing it as pointing beyond the human relationship it describes to some spiritual reality. The relationship of the husband and wife in the Song often has been interpreted as an allegory of the relationship between God and Israel or between Christ and the church.

Although the allegorical interpretation perhaps has been the most commonly held view through the centuries, there is no consensus on this. In fact, there are many descriptions in the book that do not easily fit the idea of an allegory, and it is unsatisfactory to pick and choose lyrics to apply allegorically while ignoring others. In short, there is no reason given in the book to see it as anything other than a biblical picture of what God intended human, sexual love to be.

The Song of Songs, then, recounts a story of love, marital passion, and pleasure, and it is sexual in nature. Christians readily—and correctly—declare sex as holy and a special gift from God. Indeed, the Song provides a rich source of educational information that will greatly enhance the marital relationship.

Study Approach

With the background provided by the previous chapters, we shall present in this chapter an interpretation of the Song of Songs. The interpretation will differ from the more traditional approaches but will be more consistent and coherent throughout.

Christian theology is the enterprise that seeks to construct a coherent system of Christian beliefs and practices. In order to properly understand the Scriptures, a system called *exegesis* has been developed as a basis for a critical explanation or interpretation of biblical texts. Christians have different views on how to perform biblical exegesis. The most common view is the *revealed* method. *Revealed* exegesis acknowledges that God the Holy Spirit inspired the human authors of the scriptural texts; so the words of those texts convey a divine revelation. I concur with this view and believe the Bible is indeed inspired by the Holy Spirit, although the authors penned the texts using words and writing styles that were prevalent at the time of writing. The apostle Paul is of the view that the Bible *alone* is sufficient for the spiritual wisdom we need.

> *All scripture is given by inspiration of God, and is profitable for doctrine, for reproof, for correction, for instruction in righteousness: That the man of God may be perfect, thoroughly furnished unto all good works.*
> 2 Timothy 3:16–17

If the Bible is truly inspired by the Holy Spirit, then we should see cohesiveness and completeness in each book of the Bible, as well as throughout the entire Bible. Indeed, we find this in the Song of Songs.

The difficulty lies in interpreting the scriptural writings as they were written by the ancient authors using words available during their time to express things they sometimes did not know or fully understand themselves. This is because God's message was intended to reach far beyond their generation and even beyond our own to future generations. The appropriate word to describe a certain concept might not have even existed when the author recorded God's message, thus forcing the author to resort to long phrases and sentences to describe it. In addition, the words the author originally used may have changed in meaning over time. Therefore, it is imperative that we read biblical passages with this perspective and interpret them in proper context.

At times we come across passages that are hard to interpret, and they generate various views by interpreters. This may indicate that we do not fully understand the original intent of the author. Rather than simply adopting one of the interpretations as correct or most acceptable or using our own intentions and inclinations as a guide, we should consider Peter's words.

> *Knowing this first, that no prophecy of the scripture is of one's own interpretation. For the prophecy came not in old time by the will of man: but holy*

> *men of God spoke as they were moved by the Holy Spirit.*
> *2 Peter 1:20–21*

We should be willing to say, "I do not understand" or "I do not have the answer." Admitting we do not have the answer is not a "defeat." It is plain honesty. Ask any true scientist, and he will readily admit that he does not know everything, even in his own domain of expertise. No one knows the whole Bible exhaustively. There are many reasons for this. For one, our sinful nature affects our mind, spirit, emotions, and intellect, limiting our ability to be 100 percent accurate and to be able to fully understand an author's intent. Also, we are physically confined to a time slot on this earth and cannot possibly see into the future or go back in time. We can base our knowledge only on the earthly records currently available. In addition, many scientific discoveries are yet to be made, and many treasures of the ancients are still locked underground.

It is also possible that God does not want to reveal certain things yet because the time is not ripe. When the time is ripe, God will reveal them to his sons and daughters. Until then, we shall wait. Of course, that does not mean we wait idly. We must continue to explore the treasures of the Bible, for he always has something for us. And unless we explore, we will never discover.

To recap, these are the two assumptions we are making in our study of Solomon's Song.

The Bible is inspired by the Holy Spirit.

The authors wrote the passages using words and styles available and prevalent at the time of writing.

With these two points as a starting place, the approach adopted in this book—and specifically in this chapter on the interpretation of Song of Songs—is then a matter of applying commonsense and logical reasoning. These are the principles.

Semantics and the meaning of words. We should be aware that the author lived in a different time, and the meaning of his words may have changed. Also, a word in one context may have a different meaning from the same word used in a different context or by a different author. We always have to interpret Scripture in view of its context. We must not lose sight of the purpose of the passage in general. Often the Bible explains itself, either in another passage or even in the same passage but at a different place in the passage. We cannot rely solely on dictionaries to define the meaning of a word used in the Bible, because dictionaries reflect current word usage, which may not necessarily coincide with the meaning during the time of the author. For example, in the eyes of God, when an unmarried man has a sexual relationship with an unmarried woman, they are considered married, even though they have not performed any marital ritual or ceremony or registered with local officials.

Background knowledge. The Bible provides only minimum knowledge of the culture and customs of the authors' times. The interpreter should have some additional background knowledge from other sources, such as reliable historical records. In general, a good interpreter should at least be acquainted with the Jewish language, culture, beliefs, and practices at the time of the biblical writing. This is especially true of the Old Testament. Even for most of the New Testament writings, we need to know and understand what was happening in the first century when they were written. What prompted the apostle Paul to write a letter to the Corinthians, for example? We need to know the surrounding problems of the time, as well as the customs, laws, and practices of that era. We should not read the letter merely at face value, as many attempt to do. Unless and until we can read the letter as a Corinthian of the first century did, we are unable to fully appreciate Paul's words.

Literary genre. It is universally recognized among the Christian communities that the Bible contains a variety of literary genres, each of which has certain peculiar characteristics. In fact, the individual books of the Bible are grouped together according to these genres. For example, in the Old Testament, the first five books of the Bible are called the Pentateuch (Genesis—Deuteronomy); the next twelve books are historical books (Joshua—Esther); the next five books are poetic (Job—Song of Songs); the next five books are major prophets (Isaiah—Daniel); and the next twelve books are minor prophets (Hosea—Malachi). Similarly, in the New Testament, we have the four Gospels (Matthew-John); one historical book (Acts); thirteen Pauline epistles (Romans-Hebrews); eight general epistles (Hebrews-Jude); and, finally, one prophetic book (Revelation).

Recognizing the genre of a book helps us to make better judgments in interpretation. For example, Solomon's Song of Songs is poetic, and in poetry we expect to find poetic devices such as metaphors, euphemisms, and similes used.

Scriptures do not contradict. Since the Bible is inspired by the same (and only) God throughout the ages, he is its ultimate author. Therefore, we naturally would expect there to be no contradictions in the Scriptures. Any perceived contradictions indicate that the interpretations are incorrect or imperfect, or the time is not ripe yet, or the passage is still sealed up to our understanding. We have already dealt with some of these cases, and we will see more when we study Solomon's Song.

Bible versions. There are many different versions of the Bible—the King James Version, New International Version, and New King James Version, to name just a few. No one translation of the original Scriptures can be considered 100 percent accurate in conveying the meanings completely. This is a well-known problem with translations, not only of Scripture but also of other literature as well. I consider the King James Version (KJV) to be the most reliable and the closest we can get to the original text. We have been quoting the KJV throughout this book up to now. However, for the study of Solomon's Song, we will be using the New King James Version (NKJV), along with the KJV, for reasons that will be explained later in this chapter.

PROLOGUE

Many find that the Song of Songs is a difficult book to understand. To some, it is merely a love story between King Solomon and a Shulamite woman. To others, it is a pure spiritual allegory with absolutely no human connection. Still to others, it is a song of romantic relationship between King Solomon and the Shulamite, serving also as an anecdotal allegory of a spiritual romance between Christ and the church. Some suggest it is a collection of love poems. And some see in it messianic overtones, with the state of the Fall being reversed; for example, the state of woman whose "desire shall be to your husband" (Genesis 3:16) is reversed to "his desire is toward me" (Song of Songs 7:10). What seems certain, however, is that it is still a love story between a husband and his wife; and it is a book that exalts sex as a holy expression of love.[78]

The wife is identified as a Shulamite (6:13), that is, a woman from the town of Shulem, or Shunem, in Israel. The opening verse seems to identify the husband as King Solomon.

The song of songs, which is Solomon's.
Song of Songs 1:1

Some have argued that "which is Solomon's" should be translated "which is of Solomon," while others prefer "which is for Solomon." Thus, King Solomon could be either the author or the audience. Some even suggest that it is the Shulamite, his wife, who

Physical Intimacy: A Biblical Picture

wrote it for him. And still others suggest the book was written by many authors.

As we have said, there are many interpretations of the book. We will not deal with all the various theories. Instead, we will let the text interpret itself, with the Bible providing the background knowledge.

We all agree that the Song of Songs is a love story. However, many of the verses are obscure and hard to make sense of because they are written metaphorically, and the meaning appears to be purposely concealed in various parts of the Song. Certain metaphors are themselves concealed further, such that we do not even realize they are actually hinting at something else. These metaphors often are explained or their meanings hinted at in another part of the Song. That means we must go backward and forward many times throughout the book in order to understand their meanings. To reduce burdening the reader with such repetitions, we shall first present some of the metaphors employed in the Song, with their decoded meanings.

A POEM AND A PLAY

Without a doubt, Song of Songs is a poem written in the form of a play, immersing the reader in its intimate atmosphere of bliss and passion, delights and appeals, and presenting continual and, at times, dramatic changes of events. It is about a romantic love between a husband and his wife, a Shulamite. The Song does not identify the husband directly, but we do know he was a king, and, as we will see later, we know that the king is actually King Solomon. However, we will just refer to him as "the beloved" or "the king" to avoid unnecessary theological analysis.

PRELUDE

Besides the king and the Shulamite, there are other speakers and spectators who provide the "sideshows," or preludes, that are interjected between the dialogs of the two main players. These preludes serve several purposes. They are used to camouflage certain metaphors so that the readers are distracted from the real meaning of the play. They are also used as a means of connecting one event to the next. For the most part, we will skip over these preludes and focus on the main play. However, there are some sideshows that provide a hint about certain events that are missing in the main play, and we will not omit such cases.

The New King James Version (NKJV) has identified the players (narrators) at the beginning of each dialog. This, of course, is not in the original text. These people are identified according to the number, gender, and person of the Hebrew words.[79] We will follow the NKJV's identification of the speakers, saving us time in determining who said what. We also quote the NKJV in some verses for its better poetic presentation.

We have rendered certain words and phrases in gray type instead of the usual black, to indicate that these are not in the original text so that the readers are aware of this. In some cases, reading without these grayed words paints a different picture.

A PLAY WITHIN A PLAY

It was taboo in ancient times, not only in Israel but also in many parts of the world, to mention the private parts of the body or anything erotic or sexual, such as sexual thoughts and feelings. It was doubly taboo for a woman to describe or mention her own sexual feelings. We will find that in Song of Songs euphemism is employed for the private parts, and tactics are used to disguise the sexual feelings of the woman. For example, if the woman wanted to describe her own sexual feelings, she would describe someone else's.

In the song, a storyline often is made for these euphemistic objects in such a way that a superficial story flows from one episode to the next while the underlying, true story remains obvious to someone who recognizes the metaphors but hidden to others. The meanings of these metaphors often are hinted at further along in the storyline. There are three types of euphemistic expressions in the book: those directly related to the couple, those that provide a means to create a storyline and present a surface-level description of the play, and those used as love expressions by the couple.

We need to stay focused on the underlying storyline. The story is about the love of a husband and his virgin wife on their first night. The euphemisms amplify their sexual expressions. Many of these expressions serve as educational tools to guide and enhance a married couple's sexual relationship and bond building.

As a series of sequels, the play continues from one episode to the next in a continuous and seamless manner. The seemingly effortless display of sexual expressions in wave after wave for the whole night is difficult for anyone to imitate. The reader thus is reminded and forewarned that this is a play. In my opinion, joining the episodes together is a necessity but does not reflect a reality in life. More likely, in real life, the episodes would have been performed over a period of many nights, or even months and years. How long does it take for a man to get acquainted with his new wife? Moses reckons one year.

> *When a man has taken a new wife, he shall not go out to war, neither shall he be charged with any business: but he shall be free at home one year, and shall bring happiness to his wife whom he has taken.*
> *Deuteronomy 24:5*

MOSAIC LAWS

Whether the Song of Songs is written by King Solomon, about Solomon, or for Solomon, one thing is certain: King Solomon was well versed in the law of Moses. We would expect the laws concerning love and intimacy to be strictly complied with in the play.

VINEYARD

The words *vineyard* and *garden* are used many times in the Song. At times they seem to refer metaphorically to the body, but most of the time they refer to the intimate parts of the body.

MOTHER

The word *mother* is mentioned several times in the Song, such as in verses 3:4 and 3:11. From 8:2, we will learn that "mother" is an instructor. The lyrics seem to imply that the expression of sexual love is a continual learning process. There are lessons to be learned and mastered. Skills are to be acquired, and intimate knowledge of the spouse needs to be accumulated.

CIRCUMCISION

Since the Song is either about Solomon, for Solomon, or by Solomon, we can safely assume that the king in the Song was circumcised according to the Abrahamic, or *milah,* ritual.

I assume all Christians agree that foreplay in sexual expression is allowed, and it is clearly depicted in the Song. Thus, I also assume that oral sex is not forbidden. I cannot imagine how a wife could express her desires and arouse her husband sufficiently and sustain him enough during the course of foreplay without resorting to using her mouth. The exposed glans of the circumcised is too sensitive for the use of other means, such as the hands, for stimulation. In today's environment, we can resort to using artificial lubricants. In those ancient days, there was no such luxury. Oil might not be readily available or even suitable for such a purpose.

The Song

We will now begin our discussion of the Song of Songs. We will list the lyrics part by part, with the discussion immediately following.

The song of songs, which is Solomon's.
1:1

The Shulamite:
Let him kiss me with the kisses of his mouth:
for your love is better than wine.
1:2

Because of the fragrance of your good ointments
your name is as ointment poured forth,
therefore do the virgins love you.
1:3

Draw me,
The Daughters of Jerusalem:
we will run after you:
The Shulamite:
the king has brought me into his chambers:
The Daughters of Jerusalem:
we will be glad and rejoice in you,
we will remember your love more than wine:
The Shulamite:
the upright love you.

1:4

I am dark, but lovely, O you daughters of Jerusalem,
as the tents of Kedar,
as the curtains of Solomon.
1:5

Do not look upon me, because I am dark,
Because the sun has tanned me.
My mother's sons were angry with me;
They made me the keeper of the vineyards,
But my own vineyard I have not kept.
1:6 (NKJV)

Verse 1 is the title of the Song, and we have discussed this already. Verses 2 and 3 introduce the Shulamite bride as longing for her lover and his kisses. Here we see her, as we frequently do, taking the initiative to express her desires. In verse 5 and elsewhere, the "virgins" are referred to as the "daughters of Jerusalem". They are the unmarried female friends of the Shulamite and often speak in the preludes.

In verse 4, "his chambers" refers to the king's bedrooms. It was customary for a king to have many chambers. Of course, these chambers were quite spacious and luxurious. At this point in time, the couple were at the main foyer, or entrance, to the chambers.

In verses 5 and 6, the focus changes to the Shulamite. With a degree of humbleness before the king, she introduces herself as one who is not worth all the attention of her lover. Later we will learn that "vineyard" actually refers to the intimate part of the body. Hence, here we may deduce that she is hinting that she is about to lose her virginity. In my opinion, her brothers (mother's sons) getting angry is a tactic of concealing, or camouflaging, the next sentence about her losing her virginity. In ancient times it was customary for a male—usually the father, but if the father had passed away, the sons—to take charge as guardians of the females of the household. This custom prevailed not only in Israel but also among the Palestinians and other cultures. Genesis 24 describes the story of Abraham sending his oldest servant to his homeland to get a wife for his son Isaac. The negotiation of the marriage was between the servant and the girl's brother and mother, although apparently the girl, Rebekah, was consulted. The Shulamite's brothers "made [her] the keeper of the vineyards," probably meaning they had made her the guardian of the maids in the house.

> *(To Her Beloved):*
> *Tell me, O you whom I love,*
> *Where you feed your flock,*
> *Where you make it rest at noon.*
> *For why should I be as one who veils herself*
> *By the flocks of your companions?*
> *1:7 (NKJV)*

Recall that the couple were now at the foyer to the chambers. The Shulamite asked in which chamber the king wanted to spend the night and where she could unveil herself. Comparing herself to his companions who lived in those other chambers, she was the only one still veiled, and she desired to unveil before the king. "Your flock" and "at noon" are, of course, metaphorical. At this point in time, it is night. The writer had to use "noon" simply because of the flocks in the story. So, the whole of verse 7 could be interpreted this way: "Tell me, O you whom I love, in which chamber would you spend the night? Where would you rest me? Why should I wait any longer to unveil myself?" Unveiling herself could be a reference to her consummation.

> *The Beloved:*
> *If you do not know,*
> *O fairest among women,*
> *Follow in the footsteps of the flock,*
> *And feed your little goats*
> *Beside the shepherds' tents.*
> *1:8 (NKJV)*
>
> *I have compared you, O my love,*
> *to a mare of Pharaoh's chariots.*
> *1:9*
>
> *Your cheeks are lovely with rows of jewels,*
> *your neck with chains of gold.*
> *1:10*

The reply from the beloved, "O fairest among women," affirmed that in his eyes she was the most beautiful, thus countering her humility. The meaning of "follow in the footsteps of the flock" and "feed your little goats beside the shepherds' tents" is not clear. The comparison of the Shulamite's cheeks and neck to the "mare of Pharaoh's chariots" gives us a hint of many such similes and metaphors in latter verses. After the passionate kissing, the king had started to express his admiration of the different parts of her body, beginning with the cheeks and neck.

Daughters of Jerusalem:
We will make you ornaments of gold
with studs of silver.
1:11

The Shulamite:
While the king sits at his table,
my perfume sends forth its fragrance.
1:12

A bundle of myrrh is my beloved unto me;
he shall lie all night between my breasts.
1:13

My beloved is unto me as a cluster of henna blossoms
in the vineyards of Engedi.
1:14

"At his table"[iii] takes the lead from the word "feed" in verse 7 ("feed your flock"). Three thousand years ago, there were no tables. Instead, the Jews reclined on couches for their meals. Of course, there was no

---

[iii] Some versions of the Bible translate "table" as "couch."

reason the king would want to have a meal and rest on the couple's first night in the chamber. Therefore, the king was either at the bedside or in bed, while his wife presumably was lying down (taking the hint at the word "rest" in verse 7). Verses 13 and 14 describe her wishes, desires, and perhaps her fantasies. She described her husband as if he were a bundle of myrrh and cluster of henna. Myrrh is a scent-exuding gum from a shrub native to south Arabia and Ethiopia, and henna is a bush with orange blossoms used for perfume and hair dye. The "perfume," or spikenard, in verse 12 is an aromatic ointment derived from a Himalayan herb. Comparing the king to fragrant myrrh and henna is a hint that he was highly excited. But while the king was at the bedside, who was giving out fragrance? It was the Shulamite whose "perfume" was sending forth fragrance (verse 12). Taking the cue from this, verses 13 and 14 are not describing what the king was like but rather what he was doing. He was caressing her chest and various parts of her body so that she was feeling the arousal—hence the fragrance.

> *The Beloved:*
> *Behold, you are fair, my love;*
> *behold, you are fair; you have doves' eyes.*
> *1:15*

> *The Shulamite:*
> *Behold, you are handsome, my beloved,*
> *yea, pleasant: also our bed is green.*
> *1:16*

> *The beams of our house are cedar,*

> *and* our rafters of fir.
> 1:17
>
> I *am* the rose of Sharon,
> *and* the lily of the valleys.
> 2:1

The foreplay and exchanges of admiration continue from the passions and desires of the previous scene. The king reassured his wife that she was beautiful and her eyes attractive, like doves' eyes. Her response was that he was handsome, which is a masculine way of saying he was "fair." Note that immediately after this, her focus changed yet again, as she began to describe other objects such as the bed, beams, and rafters. We will find many such instances where part of the description relates to a person or activity and the rest to something else, or vice versa. In fact, this is the author's deliberate use of metaphorical expression to describe the same person or action. In this case, the Shulamite was admiring her husband, and the bed, beams, and rafters referred to parts of his body. In this instance, it is hard to figure out what these parts are, although in some later examples, we can deduce their meaning from the surrounding context.

Sharon is the large coastal plain in Israel, stretching from Haifa and Mount Carmel in the north to the Yarkon River in the south, at the edge of the present city of Tel Aviv. It is renowned for its majesty and beauty, as it is carpeted with beautiful wildflowers and lush vegetation. The exact identities of the rose of

Sharon and the lily of the valleys are not known. Most scholars believe the rose refers to the narcissus, which covers the plains of Sharon in November. The lily might be the lotus, or water lily. Earlier, the Shulamite referred to herself as tanned dark by the sun and hence not a fair lady. With the praises of her beloved and trust in him, she had now gained confidence and felt that she actually was a beautiful rose in the plain of Sharon and a lily in the valley.

The Beloved:
As the lily among thorns,
so is my love among the daughters.
2:2

The Shulamite:
As the apple tree among the trees of the wood,
so is my beloved among the sons.
I sat down under his shadow with great delight,
and his fruit was sweet to my taste.
2:3

In the eyes of the king, her comparison of herself to a rose and lily still undervalued her beauty. Comparing her with other women was like comparing a lily to thorns. In his eyes, she was not an average woman. She responded by comparing him to an apple tree among all the non-fruit-bearing trees in the woods.

Fruits, juices, and wines have special symbolism in Solomon's Song. They are euphemisms for the intimate parts of the body. The mention of the apple tree leads to a change in the scene. She was now sitting down, "under his shadow." For that to happen, she had to be sitting at a place below him—in his shadow. The tasting of his fruit is a clear erotic reference to oral sex performed on him.

> *The Shulamite to the Daughters of Jerusalem:*
> *He brought me to the banqueting house,*
> *and his banner over me was love.*
> *2:4*
>
> *Sustain me with cakes of raisins,*
> *refresh me with apples:*
> *for I am sick with love.*
> *2:5*
>
> *His left hand is under my head,*
> *and his right hand does embrace me.*
> *2:6*
>
> *I charge you, O you daughters of Jerusalem,*
> *by the gazelles or by the hinds of the field,*
> *that you stir not up, nor awake love,*
> *till it pleases.*
> *2:7*
>
> *The Shulamite:*
> *The voice of my beloved! behold,*
> *he comes leaping upon the mountains,*
> *skipping upon the hills.*
> *2:8*

"Banqueting house" was a house of feasting, where fruits and wines were common features. Again, we see in verse 4 that the Shulamite was expressing her

Physical Intimacy: A Biblical Picture

desires as if they were the king's desires. She was projecting her desires upon him. Thus, this is not about his "drinking" and eating "fruit" and expressing his love for her. It is about her "drinking" and "eating" and engaging in her love expressions, taking the cue from the previous verse.

Continuation of the oral sexual intimacy ultimately leads to the final stages, culminating in ejaculation. In fact, this was the Shulamite's intention, as indicated in verse 4. "Sustain" and "refresh" are expressions of yearning in anticipation of receiving the ultimate goal of her burning desire ("sick with love") to please him by catapulting him to the highest bliss possible.

Verses 6 and 7 describe the progression toward this ultimate bliss. However, verse 6 describes the king's sexual expressions instead of the Shulamite's. By now we are well aware that this is because of the taboo for her to describe her own feelings and expressions. In fact, these two verses are descriptions of lovemaking performed by the king. They are borrowed from chapter 8 of the play, where the king was making love to the Shulamite. The lyrics are presented here as if they were all about the king's feelings and expressions when they are really about the *Shulamite's expressions* and the *king's feelings*. Later we will learn that verse 6 actually describes a sequence of activities that increases the receiver's state of sexual excitement in the plateau phase. This was what the author intended to convey here. Verse 7 depicts her awareness of his heightened sensations. "Stir not up, nor awake love" is a common lyric in the

Song, expressing the feelings of the beginning of orgasm. This can happen at any point in time during the plateau phase. However, in this case her intention was to bring him right to ejaculation (2:5). As if making great effort to help him cool down his elevated bliss, she uttered a vow ("I charge you"), sealing her oath on the "gazelles" (antelope) and "hinds" (deer), and passionately waited for his next response. "Stir not up" indicates she waited motionless, without adding further stimulation. She was determined not to arouse ("awaken") him until his orgasm was over ("till it pleases" him). Verse 8 describes his heightened excitement and passions as he ejaculated. Again the description is more appropriate for lovemaking than oral sex. We will revisit these lyrics again in the last chapter of the Song, where the meaning will be clearer.

My beloved is like a gazelle or a young stag:
behold, he stands behind our wall,
he looks forth through the windows,
showing himself through the lattice.
2:9

My beloved spoke, and said unto me,
Rise up, my love, my fair one,
and come away.
2:10

For, lo, the winter is past,
the rain is over and gone;
2:11

The flowers appear on the earth;

the time of singing has come,
and the voice of the turtledove
is heard in our land;
2:12

The fig tree puts forth its green figs,
and the vines with the tender grapes
give a good smell.
Arise, my love, my fair one,
and come away.
2:13

O my dove, in the clefts of the rock,
in the secret places of the cliff,
let me see your face,
let me hear your voice;
for sweet is your voice,
and your countenance is lovely.
2:14

The scene has changed. The Shulamite described her husband as a gazelle or a young stag, implying he was youthful and full of energy and fresh. "Windows" is her eyes, and "lattice" refers to her eyelashes. This may imply they were having a rest and she was dozing off. "Rise up" was his call to her to wake her up, for he had rested enough ("winter is past" and "rain is over"). This vindicates the earlier deduction that the king was experiencing ejaculation. Resting is the necessary part of the resolution period. With the sexual pressure released, he was refreshed ("flowers appear") and ready for the next episode ("time of singing has come"). It is well known that turtledoves, or pigeons, make lots of noise during courtship and mating, a hint the king was ready for love play again, as he began to dwell on her face (verse 14).

Her Brothers:
Catch us the foxes,
the little foxes, that spoil the vines:
for our vines have tender grapes.
2:15

The Shulamite:
My beloved is mine, and I am his:
he feeds his flock among the lilies.
2:16

Until the day breaks,
and the shadows flee away,
turn, my beloved,
and be like a gazelle
or a young stag
upon the mountains of Bether.
2:17

In the sideshow, the brothers wanted to capture the foxes, implying the king was the fox who took away their sister. They faced immediate rebuke from their sister, the Shulamite, who responded with the popular lyric, "My beloved is mine, and I am his." This underscored the mutual inclusiveness of the lovers and the exclusiveness to all outsiders. In verse 16, the words "his flock" are added in the KJV 2000 but are not in the Hebrew text. Reading without these words implies that he was actually feeding himself, perhaps from the kisses and erotic caresses of the Shulamite. She was telling her brothers, no, he was not the fox and she wanted to be with him.

From her shyness at the beginning of the play, she opened up to more adventurous ideas. She enjoyed every moment of the erotic journey and wanted to extend it throughout the night until daybreak. "Turn" probably means, "turn to me." It seems she was seeking the full attention of the king. Now that he was refreshed and ready, she longed to have intimate union with him. Since he already had had his turn, wasn't it logical that she now have hers? We will delay the explanation of "gazelle," "stag," and "mountains" till later, but the expression simply means she wanted the consummation of the marriage, as she was still a virgin at this point. She wanted to make love.

Before we continue, a question arises that we need to explain. Since now there was seminal emission from the oral sex, wouldn't continuation of sexual activities contravene the Mosaic law in Leviticus 15:18 or even 15:16?

> *The woman also with whom man shall lie and have an emission of semen, they shall both bathe themselves in water, and be unclean until the evening.*
> *Leviticus 15:18*
> *And if any man's semen go out from him, then he shall wash all his flesh in water, and be unclean until the evening.*
> *Leviticus 15:16*

Leviticus 15:18 deals with the case of sexual intercourse. In this case the couple have so far engaged only in oral sex. Therefore verse 18 does not apply. "Sustain me with cakes of raisins, refresh me with apples" in Song of Songs 2:5 implies that the Shulamite was prepared and looked forward to receiving his semen. If that was the case, then it may be considered that there was no semen gone out of the body. Furthermore, we will learn later in the Song that in fact the body of the Shulamite belonged to the king. This echoes the union of Adam and Eve as one.

> *A man shall . . . be joined to his wife, and they shall become one flesh.*
> *Genesis 2:24 (NKJV)*

They were not two bodies but one. Since there was no semen outside the body, then it appears Leviticus 15:16 is not applicable. The Jews followed the laws and commandments to the letter. It was thus important that the couple were seen as not contravening these laws. The Shulamite had gone to great length to ensure that they complied with these laws. In today's environment, whether a couple opts to comply with these laws literally, in spirit, or not at all is up to the individuals. More important is the lesson for the wife to learn to proactively engage in helping the husband to reach his goals.

> *The Shulamite:*
> *By night on my bed I sought him whom my soul loves:*
> *I sought him, but I found him not.*
> *3:1*

> *I will rise now, and go about the city*

in the streets, and in the squares
I will seek him whom my soul loves:
I sought him, but I found him not.
3:2

The watchmen that go about the city found me:
to whom I said, *Saw you him whom my soul loves?*
3:3

It was but a little after I passed by them,
when I found him whom my soul loves:
I held him, and would not let him go,
until I had brought him into my mother's house,
and into the chamber of her that conceived me.
3:4

I charge you, O you daughters of Jerusalem,
by the gazelles or by the hinds of the field,
that you stir not up, nor awake my love,
till it pleases.
3:5

Continuing from 2:17, the couple were just starting the second episode when it seemed suddenly the king "disappeared" into the night and his bride had to look for him in the dark. This is a very unusual scenario, especially considering this was their first night together. Why did he suddenly "disappear" into the city when he had an important duty to perform: the consummation of the marriage? It is highly unlikely he was afraid or had lost interest in her. Instead, it seems the king and the Shulamite had never left their bed. The "streets," "squares," and "watchmen" are "red herrings" in the story. However, they do convey certain meaning for the underlying storyline. Clearly, she was searching for something ("him whom my soul loves"). Thus, the underlying story is that while the king was admiring her face, she was searching "him" out but was having difficulty finding what she was looking for.

As mentioned before, in many ancient cultures—and the Jews were no exception—it was taboo for a female to refer directly to the genitals of either sex. Euphemistic objects and phrases were used instead. We know it was at night, and it was dark. In those days there was no electricity, and even if there was a fireplace, the chamber was still dark. The clue to understanding her words is that when she eventually found what she was looking for ("him whom my soul loves"), she held him tightly and brought him to the "house" and then into the "chamber." Of course, after she had found "him," she did not literally bring "him" to her mother's house for the consummation. There are two metaphors here, the "house" and the "chamber," and the two are connected. First, he had to enter the "house" and then the "chamber." The word "conceived" is a giveaway, hinting that these metaphors relate to lovemaking. We will see that the next few verses (beginning at verse 6) describe the male genitals, and not the consummation we might be expecting. Thus, the "house" is not the opening of the vagina but the lips, or mouth; and the "chamber" is not the vagina but the cavity of the mouth. It is clear, then, that in the dark she was searching for his penis ("him whom my soul loves"), perhaps using her hand; and when she found it, she went down and performed oral sex again. "Mother" indicates that the oral sex she was performing requires knowledge and skills and that she had learned the techniques, whatever they might be. He had just ejaculated, so now she was arousing him again to prepare him for the consummation.

Again, in verse 5 we see the familiar lyrics (see 2:7), which in this context simply mean he was close to orgasm. The words in 2:8 are not repeated, however, indicating he did not experience ejaculation this time. The next few verses (3:6–11) explain why there was no ejaculation.

> *The Shulamite:*
> *Who is this that comes out of the wilderness*
> *like pillars of smoke,*
> *perfumed with myrrh and frankincense,*
> *with all the fragrant powders of the merchant?*
> *3:6*
>
> *Behold the couch, which is Solomon's;*
> *threescore valiant men are about it,*
> *of the valiant of Israel.*
> *3:7*
>
> *They all hold swords,*
> *being expert in war:*
> *every man has his sword upon his thigh*
> *because of fear in the night.*
> *3:8*
>
> *King Solomon made himself a chariot*
> *of the wood of Lebanon.*

Secrets of First Love

> *He made its posts of silver,*
> *its base of gold,*
> *the covering of its seat of purple,*
> *its interior being paved with love,*
> *by the daughters of Jerusalem.*
> 3:10
>
> *Go forth, O you daughters of Zion,*
> *and behold king Solomon with the crown*
> *with which his mother crowned him*
> *on the day of his wedding,*
> *and on the day of the gladness of his heart.*
> 3:11

"Who is this that comes out of the wilderness" is a lead-in phrase, introducing something that is worthy of attention. It is equivalent to saying, "Who is this coming from nowhere?" What follows is a mystery we need to solve.

"Myrrh and frankincense" and "fragrant powders" describe this mysterious "pillars of smoke." This is followed by a long narrative about King Solomon's couch, together with Israel's valiant men. This leads back to King Solomon himself and the crown given to him by his "mother," specifically for his wedding. What could this crown be?

The Shulamite had just finished giving the king an erotic arousal session, using her month and lips. What she was seeing, of course, were his genitals. "Who is this?" she exclaimed. The "crown" was his glans, as he was circumcised. Following that, the "pillars of smoke" refer to his pubic hair. "Mother" refers to techniques the king had learned in relation to the "crown." The "couch" and the "chariot" is the place where "King Solomon" sits, a sure reference to the pubic and surrounding areas. And "King Solomon" himself is a reference to the phallus. The important message from these lyrics is that there are techniques concerning the phallus and the glans that a husband needs to learn. And the king had done well, for he did not ejaculate.

> *The Beloved:*
> *Behold, you are fair, my love;*
> *behold, you are fair;*
> *you have doves' eyes behind your veil:*
> *your hair is like a flock of goats,*
> *going down from mount Gilead.*
> *4:1*
>
> *Your teeth are like a flock of sheep that are even shorn,*
> *which came up from the washing;*
> *every one of which bears twins,*
> *and none is barren among them.*
> *4:2*
>
> *Your lips are like a thread of scarlet,*
> *and your mouth is lovely:*
> *your temples are like a piece of pomegranate*
> *behind your veil.*
> *4:3*
>
> *Your neck is like the tower of David*

built for an armory,
on which there hang a thousand shields,
all shields of mighty men.
4:4

Your two breasts are like two fawns,
twins of a gazelle,
which feed among the lilies.
4:5

Until the day breaks,
and the shadows flee away,
I will go up to the mountain of myrrh,
and to the hill of frankincense.
4:6

You are all fair, my love;
there is no spot in you.
4:7

Come with me from Lebanon, my spouse,
with me from Lebanon:
look from the top of Amana,
from the top of Shenir and Hermon,
from the lions' dens,
from the mountains of the leopards.
4:8

You have ravished my heart,
my sister, my spouse;
you have ravished my heart
with one look of your eyes,
with one jewel of your necklace.
4:9

How fair is your love, my sister, my spouse!
how much better is your love than wine!
and the fragrance of your perfume than all spices!
4:10

Your lips, O my spouse,
drop like the honeycomb:
honey and milk are under your tongue;
and the fragrance of your garments is like the
fragrance of Lebanon.
4:11

A garden enclosed is my sister, my spouse;
a spring shut up, a fountain sealed.
4:12

Your plants are an orchard of pomegranates,
with pleasant fruits; henna, with spikenard,
4:13

Spikenard and saffron;
calamus and cinnamon,
with all trees of frankincense;
myrrh and aloes,
with all the chief spices:
4:14

A fountain of gardens,
a well of living waters,
and streams from Lebanon.
4:15

With the help of the Shulamite, the king was now empowered again. Continuing where he had left off (caressing and admiring her face), he described the beauty of her eyes, hair, head ("mount Gilead"), mouth, lips, temples, neck, and then, farther down, the breasts. There he echoed her desires "until the day breaks and the shadows flee away." Note that when the Shulamite declared her desire for intimacy for the whole night, her focus was on giving him erotic love. When the king now declared his desires for the whole night, he wanted it for her.

Later we will learn that "mountain of myrrh" and "hill of frankincense" refer to her labia majora (outer lips) and labia minora (inner lips) respectively. "You are fair" is repeated many times, reaffirming his intense admiration of her. Looking at her from various angles, he declared that her features "ravished [his] heart." Verse 11 describes his erotic fantasies and admiration of her genitals, as sweet and fragrant as the dripping honey and milk. "Under your tongue" probably refers to the area beneath her inner lips.

As if suddenly awakened to reality, he realized she was still a virgin (verse 12). "A garden enclosed," "a spring shut up," and "a fountain sealed" depict her virginity as whole and intact. Referring to her vulva as "an orchard of pomegranates," he went on to admire and caress it, describing its beauty in vivid details in verses 14 and 15. "A fountain of gardens," "a well of living waters," and "streams from Lebanon" all seem to refer to the closed spring and sealed fountain in verse 12, and hint at his desire to unseal, or unblock, her and arouse her like water and streams, figuratively meaning "plenty of fluids." He was, of course, expressing his desire to perform the consummation and to give her orgasms.

> *The Shulamite:*
> *Awake, O north wind;*
> *and come, you south;*
> *blow upon my garden,*
> *that its spices may flow out.*
> *Let my beloved come into his garden,*
> *and eat its pleasant fruits.*
> *4:16*

The call for the wind to blow upon "my garden" hints at her escalating passions in response to his caresses and stimulations and also resonates with his desire to pleasure her. "My garden" refers to her vulva. Spices do not flow, yet she wished her "spices" to flow out from her "garden," hinting more directly of her desire that her arousal fluids would flow.

There is a twist in the next line: "let my beloved come into his garden." She referred to "her garden" as "his garden." At this point, she decided it was high time she submitted her body to him; hence, "her garden" became "his garden." She invited him to "eat" the fruits of his "garden." "Eat its pleasant fruits" refers to oral sex. Note that the oral sex was performed on her external genitals only, as the lyrics so far do not refer to any of her other organs.

> *The Beloved:*
> *I have come into my garden, my sister, my spouse:*
> *I have gathered my myrrh with my spice;*

> *I have eaten my honeycomb with my honey;*
> *I have drunk my wine with my milk:*
> *(To His Friends)*
> *eat, O friends;*
> *drink, yea, drink abundantly, O beloved.*
> *5:1*

The king accepted her submission and assumed the leadership role. She had initiated the love play and assisted him in preparation for the leadership role. Now she was prepared to submit to him. To submit is to please. To lead is to serve. To submit means the woman is to let go of herself, to trust her husband, to trust her own body, to feel naked without shame in front of her husband, and to express her own feelings without faking. To lead means the husband is to unselfishly care for the needs of his wife, to understand his wife's responses, and to sacrifice his own pleasure.

The apostle Paul commands the husband to assume the leadership role and the wife the submissive role (Ephesians 5:22–25). These roles exemplify the roles of Jesus and the church. Jesus says,

> *"For even the Son of Man [Jesus] did not come to be served, but to serve, and to give his life a ransom for many."*
> *Mark 10:45 (NKJV)*

The "gathering," "drinking," and "eating" in "my garden" all refer to the oral sex he performed on her.

The Shulamite:
I sleep, but my heart wakes:
it is the voice of my beloved that knocks, saying,
Open to me, my sister, my love,
my dove, my perfect one:
for my head is filled with dew,
and my locks with the drops of the night.
5:2

I have put off my robe;
how shall I put it on?
I have washed my feet;
how could I soil them?
5:3

My beloved put in his hand by the latch of the door,
and my heart was thrilled for him.
5:4

I rose up to open to my beloved;
and my hands dripped with myrrh,
and my fingers with sweet smelling myrrh,
upon the handles of the lock.
5:5

I opened to my beloved;
but my beloved had withdrawn himself, and was gone:
my soul failed when he spoke:
I sought him, but I could not find him;
I called him, but he gave me no answer.
5:6

The watchmen that went about the city found me,

> *they struck me, they wounded me;*
> *the keepers of the walls took away my veil from me.*

5:7

> *I charge you, O daughters of Jerusalem,*
> *if you find my beloved,*
> *that you tell him,*
> *that I am sick with love.*

5:8

There seems to be a dramatic change of event, but the king had an unfinished task yet to perform! His head and his hair were wet, perhaps from his sweat, or perhaps from her moist "garden."

Where was he, and what was he doing? He was caressing her and arousing her with his mouth. The intimacy must continue; the love must play on. He had an important task to perform.

"Open to me" was his request. And she responded, amid "reluctant" excuses, opening her "door" so that he had access inside. The Shulamite said, "My beloved put in his hand by the latch of the door." It is possible the "latch" could be what we now commonly call the G-spot, or Gräfenberg spot, even though its existence is still controversial and debatable. It is more probable, however, that it is a euphemism for her hymen. She was still a virgin! And he was preparing her for the consummation by performing what is called "vaginal stretching," or "hymen dilation," which allows the erect penis to enter more comfortably and less painfully for the bride on her first night.[80]

She responded to his thoughtfulness ("my heart was thrilled"). The word *open* was used twice. First, she opened to allow him to "put in his hand by the latch." "My hands" and "my fingers" are convenient wordplay to describe her aroused state. She was dripping with intense pleasure and ecstasies from her vulva, perhaps from the thought of a husband who was so very patient and cared about her well-being.

The second time she used the word *open* it seemed to introduce a twist of event—or did it? She was about to accept him inside ("opened to my beloved"), but he "was gone" (Song of Songs 5:6)! Would any bridegroom leave his bride at a time like that? Of course not. They were both still in the bedroom, but on the superficial expression of the storyline, the lyrics present a drama of her seeking him, of her being wounded, and of the "keepers" taking away her "veil." This was all an obvious euphemistic reference to her first sexual intercourse and loss of virginity. "Wounded" refers to her bleeding as a result of the consummation. "Veil" is her hymen, and the "keepers" refer to the king. "Tell him, that I am sick with love" says it all. She was willingly accepting this consummation and giving her virginity to him.

> *The Daughters of Jerusalem:*
> *What is your beloved more than another beloved,*
> *O you fairest among women?*
> *what is your beloved more than another beloved,*
> *that you so charge us?*
> *5:9*
>
> *The Shulamite:*

My beloved is white and ruddy,
the chiefest among ten thousand.
5:10

His head is as the most fine gold,
his locks are wavy,
and black as a raven.
5:11

His eyes are like doves by the rivers of waters,
washed with milk,
and fitly set.
5:12

His cheeks are like a bed of spices,
like sweet flowers:
his lips like lilies,
dripping sweet smelling myrrh.
5:13

His arms are as rounded gold set with beryl:
his body is as carved ivory overlaid with sapphires.
5:14

His legs are pillars of marble,
set upon bases of fine gold:
his countenance is as Lebanon,
excellent as the cedars.
5:15

His mouth is most sweet:
yea, he is altogether lovely.
This is my beloved,
and this is my friend,

O daughters of Jerusalem.
5:16

After the consummation was over, the couple took a break. The prologue of the daughters of Jerusalem provides the lead-in to the next episode. Note that the king did not continue until ejaculation. Instead, he allowed his bride a break. There is no description of her reaching orgasm either.

Again the Shulamite initiated the love play as she described her beloved from the head downward until she reached his legs in verse 15. The description depicts her admiration of his body as solid, masculine, and strong. She compared many of his features to solid substances, but not his eyes and lips, where she saw gentleness and softness.

She left the most intimate part to the last in verse 16. The "mouth" undoubtedly is a euphemism because she had already described his "lips" in verse 13. It refers to his genitals, and possibly the opening (meatus) of the glans, since this was the only part that had not been mentioned. She adored it as sweet and altogether lovely. "My friend" is a possible fond reference to the meatus.

The Daughters of Jerusalem:
Where has your beloved gone,
O you fairest among women?
where has your beloved turned aside?
that we may seek him with you.
6:1

The Shulamite:
My beloved has gone down into his garden,
to the beds of spices,
to feed his flock in the gardens,
and to gather lilies.
6:2

I am my beloved's,
and my beloved is mine:
he feeds his flock among the lilies.
6:3

By now we are convinced that "garden" always refers to the intimate parts. Since the Shulamite submitted to him (her garden is his garden), the king now had two gardens—one his own, and the other his bride's. "My beloved has gone down into his garden," therefore, should read as "my beloved has gone to my garden." It is her "garden." Again, "his flock" is not in the original text. He thus fed among the lilies. "Lilies" is a euphemistic reference to her pubic hair—a softer version of "pillars of smoke" in 3:6. He was caressing and brushing against her "lilies" to build up her passions. In 6:3, she emphasized their exclusive relationship and her pride with the bonding.

The Beloved:
You are beautiful, O my love,
as Tirzah, lovely as Jerusalem,
awesome as an army with banners.
6:4

Turn away your eyes from me,

for they have overcome me:
your hair is as a flock of goats going down from Gilead.
6:5

Your teeth are as a flock of sheep
which go up from the washing,
every one bears twins,
and there is not one barren among them.
6:6

As a piece of a pomegranate are your temples
behind your veil.
6:7

There are threescore queens,
and fourscore concubines,
and virgins without number.
6:8

My dove, my perfect one, is the only one;
she is the only one of her mother,
she is the favorite one of her that bore her.
The daughters saw her, and blessed her;
yea, the queens and the concubines,
and they praised her.
6:9

Who is she that looks forth as the morning,
fair as the moon,
clear as the sun,
and awesome as an army with banners?
6:10

The king's focus then shifted to his wife's head and her head alone. The pace had changed from an explosive, dynamic rhythm to a slower pace. As if he had missed out on some details previously, he concentrated on the minute features of her head. Intoxicated by her beauty, he compared her with all those around and came to the conclusion that she was the most beautiful—fair as the moon, clear as the sun, awesome as the banners of an army, and delightful as Tirzah. He declared that no one could match her! She was blessed!

> *The Shulamite:*
> *I went down into the garden of nuts*
> *to see the blossoms of the valley,*
> *and to see whether the vine had budded,*
> *and the pomegranates were in bloom.*
> *6:11*
>
> *Before I was aware,*
> *my desire had made me*
> *as the chariots of my noble people.*
> *6:12*

Certainly the change of mood had caught the attention of the Shulamite. Frustrated by this slow-paced interlude and lack of physical intimacy, she went down to the "garden of nuts." The "nuts" is a euphemistic reference to his testicles. The "vine" is the flaccid penis, "blossoms of the valley" is the pubic area between the legs, and the "pomegranates" are probably the scrotum. It is quite common in prolonged foreplay for the erection to wax and wane.

Hence, we quite often witness the Shulamite stimulating him to sustain the erection and his level of excitement. Her intention was very clear. She wanted to reenergize him by massaging the testicles. Before long, she found herself intoxicated and aroused by the budding "vine," and her heart pulsated like thunderous "chariots" racing. Her passions escalated. Her emotions were ecstatic.

> *The Beloved and His Friends:*
> *Return, return, O Shulamite;*
> *return, return, that we may look upon you.*
> *The Shulamite:*
> *Why will you look upon the Shulamite?*
> *As upon a dance before two armies?*
> *6:13*

As the Shulamite passionately continued with what she was doing, there came voices, saying, "Return, return." Why return? Why did the king and his friends want her to "return," and upon what did they want to "look" (or "gaze," maybe even "watch")? "Return" could mean, "come back." *The Preacher's Commentary* reckons this as a call to dancing by turning or whirling.[81] The translators of the NKJV aptly add the friends of the king in the sideshow. Here we witness a transition of moods from one of lackluster and casual existence to one of dynamic, drumbeating tempo, as the friends call for her "return" so they can watch the dancing.

Why did the king also call the Shulamite to "return"? Didn't he like her love play? Recalling his thoughts as he was caressing and admiring her face before she went down below, it was now his turn to please her. "Return, return" was a soft call from him that he was now aroused enough to resume what he was doing. He wanted to lead. He wanted to serve her.

The baffling answer from the bride has produced many scholarly discussions of what her intents actually were. An answer in the form of a rhetorical question to her beloved's soft call to return highlights her intellect and intimate understanding of his desires.

"Shulamite" is used for the first time in Song of Songs and is an obvious reference to her origin in a place famous for belly dancing. "Do you want to watch my belly dancing?" could be the question posed to the friends. "Do you want my body?" could be the unspoken but hinted question for the king. Sure enough, her question shifted the focus from her head to the rest of her body.

> *The Beloved:*
> *How beautiful are your feet in sandals,*
> *O prince's daughter!*
> *the curves of your thighs are like jewels,*
> *the work of the hands of a skillful craftsman.*
> *7:1*
>
> *Your navel is like a round goblet,*
> *which lacks not blended drink:*
> *your belly is like a heap of wheat*
> *set about with lilies.*
> *7:2*
>
> *Your two breasts are like two fawns*

that are twins of a gazelle.
7:3

Your neck is as a tower of ivory;
your eyes like the pools of Heshbon,
by the gate of Bathrabbim:
your nose is as the tower of Lebanon
which looks toward Damascus.
7:4

Your head crowns you like Carmel,
and the hair of your head is like purple;
the king is held captive by your tresses.
7:5

How fair and how pleasant are you,
O love, for your delights!
7:6

This your stature is like to a palm tree,
and your breasts to its clusters.
7:7

I said, I will go up to the palm tree,
I will take hold of its branches:
may also your breasts be as clusters of the vine,
and the fragrance of your breath like apples;
7:8

And the roof of your mouth like the best wine
The Shulamite:
for my beloved, that goes down sweetly,
flowing gently over lips and teeth.
7:9

Instead of caressing her and expressing his love from the head downward, the king chose to start at her feet and move upward—feet, thighs, and then navel. "Navel" could refer to her vulva since "goblet" is too big for a navel. "Goblet" also implies roundness. It is thus more likely a reference to her vaginal opening. This also implies that she was lying down. "Blended drink," or "beverage," implies moistness. "Lilies" again is an obvious reference to her pubic hair. From there, he moved up to the waist, neck, eyes, mouth ("gate"), nose, and finally her head and hair. "Tower of Lebanon" does not indicate a big nose but rather speaks of its elegance and appropriate position on her face. In verse 6 he again admired her features and attributes.

"Palm tree" in verse 7 describes the shape of her torso as slim, tall, and elegant. "I will go up to the palm tree" indicates the king was lying on top of her and was crawling and "climbing" upwards, arousing her senses as he moved. In Malaysia, I have seen villagers climb up coconut trees to plug coconuts. The climbing is not always in a straight line. Sometimes the climber goes in a spiraling fashion to avoid certain spikes on the tree trunk. Similarly, the king might have had to turn her body so that he could give her massages as he moved up.

Finally, he reached her upper limbs. The swirling and twisting of the two torsos provided the rhythmic and energized tempo to the "dance." "Branches" refers to her upper limbs. "I will take hold of its branches" implies that she was at the receiving end of the love play. Verses 8 and 9 describe the intimate love she received from him as she lay under him. Although he was in control, he was gentle and tender. These two verses contrast starkly with previous verses, as if now every movement were in slow motion, as dictated by the slow movements of the lips. The New Revised Standard Version (NRSV) translates "flowing gently over lips and teeth" as "gliding over lips and teeth." The lyrics leave much to the imagination, but one thing is clear: Although the Shulamite was the receiver, she was proactively engaging in the activities and enhancing their mutual feelings. The king was not the one who dictated the rhythm and direction of the play: she did so by the movements of her lips. The reason for her newfound desire is stated in the next verse.

I am my beloved's,
and his desire is toward me.
7:10

There was distinct change of theme at the point of her submission to her bridegroom in 4:16, where "my garden" became "his garden." Before her submission, she emphasized the mutual inclusiveness between them thus:

My beloved is mine, and I am his.
2:16

It was all about "me first; you second," even though they were mutually inclusive. However, the order of emphasis changed from "me first" to "you first," emphasizing her submissiveness to him. Nevertheless, the mutual inclusiveness remains.

> *I am my beloved's, and my beloved is mine.*
> 6:3

The theme then evolved further. The emphasis totally shifted to one of total emulsification of personalities into holistic oneness. There was no distinction between the two individuals.

> *I am my beloved's,*
> *and his desire is toward me.*
> 7:10

It was no more about two distinct persons, each with his and her own mind, desires, and purposes. There was only one "person" and one purpose. Both had a new, intensified, intimate desire and a new, blended, common purpose. She wanted to please him, and his goal was her goal. And his goal was to please her. The awareness of individual needs gave way to the common needs. This oneness is possible only when husband and wife are willing to imitate the love between Jesus and his church, as we learned in chapter 6. Sacrificial love is giving in love. Submissive love is receiving in love. That brings us back to Genesis 2.

> *Therefore shall a man leave his father and his mother, and shall cleave unto his wife: and they shall be one flesh.*

Genesis 2:24

Oneness is not about the mere physical or sexual union of two persons. It is a spiritual, sexual, physical, emotional, and intellectual union, such that the two are one-minded in achieving the common desire, with one leading the play while the other resonates and helps. For this common goal, the woman was created as a "helper" and not as a mate or partner.

> *And the LORD God said, It is not good that the man should be alone; I will make him a helper suitable for him.*
> *Genesis 2:18*

The wife is to help her husband achieve his desire (goal). And his desire is to please (serve) her. To serve her, he must learn to prolong his stay in the plateau phase by sacrificing his own orgasms. To help and please him, she must learn to understand him in terms of his desires, his physiological states, and his emotions and proactively engage in the play. The oneness has nothing to do with producing offspring, though that is the necessary by-product that ensures survival of the human race. "Suitable" suggests equality in their physical being, although the roles are different, as we have discussed elsewhere.

> *Come, my beloved,*
> *let us go forth into the field;*
> *let us lodge in the villages.*
> *7:11*

> *Let us get up early to the vineyards;*
> *let us see if the vine has budded,*
> *whether the grape blossoms have opened,*
> *and the pomegranates are in bloom:*
> *there will I give you my loves.*
> *7:12*

> *The mandrakes give a fragrance,*
> *and at our gates are all manner of pleasant fruits,*
> *new and old, which I have laid up for you, O my beloved.*
> *7:13*

"Field," "villages," and "vineyards" are euphemisms equivalent to "garden" and thus references to their intimate parts. We can see the purpose of their visit in the next few lyrics, which again speak euphemistically of the budding "vine," "grape blossoms," and blooming "pomegranates." She wanted to make sure both of them were fully aroused again in preparation for the next episode, which she had planned ("laid up for you"). Submissiveness is not altogether passive. As we witness here, she had a plan, an idea, and she was taking the initiative. While she would be playing a submissive role, she knew in order for her king to play the leading role, she had to help him and show him the way.

> *O that you were as my brother,*
> *that nursed at the breasts of my mother!*
> *if I should find you outside, I would kiss you;*
> *yea, I would not be despised.*

8:1

I would lead you,
and bring you into my mother's house,
who had instructed me:
I would cause you to drink of spiced wine
of the juice of my pomegranate.
8:2

(To the Daughters of Jerusalem)
His left hand is under my head,
and his right hand embraces me.
8:3

I charge you,
O daughters of Jerusalem,
that you stir not up, nor awake my love,
until it pleases.
8:4

The woman's wish that her beloved were like her "brother" was an exclamation expressing her desire that her king knew more about her anatomy, and physiology and the skills of pleasuring her.

In verse 2, the meaning of "mother" finally is revealed. She was an instructor about sex. Of course, this is a metaphorical expression indicating that sex—at least certain aspects of it—is a learning process. The Shulamite had learned from her "mother" about her sexuality, and she wanted to pass this knowledge on to her king. The lyrics in verse 2 are not about her desire to show him the techniques of how to arouse her. The king already knew about that, as we see in 4:15–5:4, for example. The next two verses (Song of Songs 8:3–4) employ the familiar lyrics of sexual intercourse, indicating it was the Shulamite's intention to guide her lover into bringing her to blissful fulfillment during sexual intercourse. That is the ultimate goal of submissiveness. It is not passively receiving but proactively engaging and aiding the husband in accomplishing his goal.

So, what did the Shulamite show her lover? The trouble is that the double taboo comes into play here. It was taboo for her to talk about her own intimate parts, and it was also taboo to describe her own sexual feelings or give advice regarding sex. Hence, the lyrics skip over this completely, moving from the expression of her intention to show him the techniques in verse 2 to the scene describing the sexual intercourse itself in verse 3. We will learn from verse 5 (later) that it was the Shulamite who was having the blissful experience and had fallen asleep. Thus from verse 3 to verse 5, the author of the Song has omitted the plateau and orgasm phases the Shulamite had experienced. And no instructions on the techniques are given.

Would it not be wonderful if she had left behind some instructions or even some hints? Indeed, the author of the Song of Songs knew its importance. The Shulamite previously had employed what we call the double entendre tactic. She needed to conceal her feelings and instruction from unsuspecting eyes. As there was no way she could describe her own sexuality and feelings directly, she instead described

Physical Intimacy: A Biblical Picture

what appeared to be somebody else's feelings and actions. An obvious choice for that somebody was her own husband. This ploy was used to describe the sexual technique she taught her king, and it was concealed . The next verse reveals where the technique was hidden, through the clue given by a relative.

> *A Relative:*
> *Who is this that comes up from the wilderness, leaning upon her beloved?*
> *I awakened you under the apple tree:*
> *there your mother brought you forth:*
> *there she brought you forth that bore you.*
> *8:5*

Again, "Who is this that comes up from the wilderness?" is a hint of a mystery to be solved: Who is this coming up from nowhere? After the sexual intercourse, a relative of the Shulamite noticed the Shulamite (or someone) was leaning against her king and woke her up. Of course, this is merely a lead-in ploy for continuation of the storyline. Apparently she was exhausted after going through the blissful experience and had fallen asleep or was taking a nap under the "apple tree." Of course, we know the couple were still in their bedroom. The familiar "apple tree" reminds us of the scene where the Shulamite performed her first oral sex on her husband (2:3). In the use of the term "mother," the relative effectively was suggesting that this one who had taught the Shulamite the techniques of oral sex also had taught her other techniques under that "apple tree." Hence, we see the phrase "brought you forth" repeated. The relative was hinting that if we were to hunt for the missing technique the Shulamite taught the king, we should look for the "apple tree." In other words, the description of sexual intercourse was actually employed in chapter 2, where the "apple tree" was.

Recall that earlier when we described the oral sex "under the tree" we skipped over the lyrics and merely presented the interpretations without explaining how we arrived at them. The lyrics actually represented the sexual expressions and feelings associated with sexual intercourse but were used to describe the equivalents in oral sex in chapter 2, that is, the foreplay (2:6), oral sex (2:7), and orgasm/ejaculation(2:8). Interestingly, some lyrics are omitted from the description of sexual intercourse here in chapter 8. The missing lyrics on lovemaking thus render the description incomplete. This is a bit like the "treasure hunt" we read about in children's storybooks or played in games. A pirate typically left behind some landscape markings and clues so that later he could find his way back to his hidden treasures. The author of the Song did something similar by posting the relative as the marker. Instead of repeating the same lyrics in chapter 8 to describe lovemaking, the author chose to leave a marker—the relative—and omit some of those lines. The storyline thus can be very confusing for the casual reader—the storyline on oral sex does not seem to make sense because of the mix of player roles, feelings, and activities and because the description is more appropriate for sexual intercourse and the lovemaking play is missing its vital scenes. As a result it is easy to misconstrue the play altogether. Both important aspects of love expressions (oral sex and sexual intercourse) and the secrets of physical love were cleverly concealed.

Let us revisit the lyrics under the apple tree in chapter 2, reproduced below. This time we shall study them in the context of chapter 8, where, as we have seen, the text hints that the lyrics apply to the two actually having sexual intercourse.

> *The Shulamite:*
> *As the apple tree among the trees of the wood,*
> *so is my beloved among the sons.*
> *I sat down under his shadow with great delight,*
> *and his fruit was sweet to my taste.*
> *2:3*
>
> *The Shulamite to the Daughters of Jerusalem:*
> *He brought me to the banqueting house,*
> *and his banner over me was love.*
> *2:4*
>
> *Sustain me with cakes of raisins,*
> *refresh me with apples:*
> *for I am sick with love.*
> *2:5*
>
> *His left hand is under my head,*
> *and his right hand does embrace me.*
>
> *2:6*
> *I charge you, O you daughters of Jerusalem,*
> *by the gazelles or by the hinds of the field,*

that you stir not up, nor awake love,
till it pleases.
2:7

The Shulamite:
The voice of my beloved! behold,
he comes leaping upon the mountains,
skipping upon the hills.
2:8

Verses 3 to 5 describe the arousal phase, as we have studied before. An obvious point of transition to increasing excitement (generally called the plateau phase) is verse 6. Since both 2:6 and 8:3 are repeating lyrics, they serve as the clue left by the relative that this is the starting point, where we will find the treasure of her technique that she wanted her king to learn.

In the plateau phase, a couple typically engages in foreplay to express their love, gradually bringing the level of excitement up to a prolonged stay there. Song of Songs 2:6 here describes a position in which the husband can give maximum excitement to his wife. The wife lies on her back (or on her right side) and he lies by her side on her right, such that her neck is resting under his left arm. In this comfortable position, he can kiss her upper body—mouth, earlobe, neck, or breasts—while his right hand is free to embrace her or reach to the lower part of her body for caressing and fondling. The focal point in this phase is to slowly build up her excitement and passions.

Physical Intimacy: A Biblical Picture

Verse 7 describes how her responses had escalated and finally she was close to orgasm. With these signals, he entered her ("Behold, he comes"). The "mountains" and the "hills" refer to her outer lips and inner lips. "Gazelles" and "hinds" are animals like the antelope and deer. We often consider the galloping (leaping and skipping) of these animals as graceful because the motions are light and gentle, almost as if in slow motion. These circular, gentle motions were the technique the Shulamite taught her lover.

We can gather from this that her husband lay on top of her and inserted inside her. He aligned his pelvic bone at the top ends of her outer lips and pressed lightly against them. He then gently did a downward stroke, following the contour of her outer lips. At the end of the stroke, he lifted up and repeated the stroking in circular, "galloping" motions ("leaping and skipping"). Meanwhile the penis was gliding in and out inside the vagina.

There are two results of this technique. First, externally, as the pelvis strokes downward along the contour of the outer lips, it stretches them downward and thus creates a pulling tension on the clitoris. At the end of the downward stroke, he lifts up and returns to the original position to start over again. This stretching and unstretching of the labia and the clitoris cause an arousal sensation.

Second, internally, the motion of the penis is much more complex as a result of the external circular motion. While the penis glides in and out inside the vagina, the glans also traces a circular motion (from posterior to anterior—similar to the action of a seesaw

), using the opening of the vagina as the pivot (the outer third of the vagina being muscular and firm) and the penis shaft as the lever. We have learned that during sexual excitement, the inner two-thirds of the vagina actually is wider than the first third, due to what is often referred to as tenting, or ballooning. Now we know why: this accommodates the circular, swinging motion of the penis glans.

Furthermore, as the penis moves in and out inside the vagina, it pulls on the inner lips, which rub against the clitoris. This is possible only with the circumcised penis (and one with short foreskin), as there is no excess foreskin, and only when the wife is fully aroused and close to orgasm. The vagina will grasp the penis shaft tightly. In the case of the uncircumcised, the vagina will be grasping on the loose foreskin, and there will be no pulling tension on the inner lips. Perhaps this is what the apostle Paul meant about the "benefits" of the circumcised.

> *For circumcision verily profits, if you keep the law: but if you are a breaker of the law, your circumcision is made uncircumcision.*
> *Romans 2:25*

Note that the circumcised husband must have a loving (circumcised) heart. Circumcision serves as a reminder of sacrificial love. The husband must be full of patience and care for the well-being of his wife. If the wife is not fully aroused, it will be a painful experience. Thus, circumcision will be worse than uncircumcision.

The lyrics introduce us to a basic understanding of a very complex technique. However, they do not tell us how the Shulamite could have proactively engaged in the play. This is left to the reader to explore further.

The technique presented here applies to the so-called missionary position, where the man is on top of the woman. Once we understand the gist of the technique, it is possible to vary and apply it to other positions. The sciences are just beginning to give us some understanding of the complexity of sexual intercourse. No wonder Agur, the son of Jakeh, in his sayings declares,

> *There are three things which are too wonderful for me, yea, four which I know not: The way of an eagle in the air; the way of a serpent upon a rock; the way of a ship in the midst of the sea; and the way of a man with a maiden.*
> *Proverbs 30:18–19*

The play now comes to a close. The profound bonding between the husband and wife has grown stronger, like a seal that glues together and like flames burning forever. Their love was exclusive to others and vindicated by their union into one flesh. No amount of wealth or anything else could replace it. The Shulamite thirsted for more of their love and longed to explore new horizons.

> *The Shulamite to Her Beloved:*
> *Set me as a seal upon your heart,*
> *as a seal upon your arm:*
> *for love is as strong as death;*

jealousy is cruel as the grave:
its flames are flames of fire,
a most vehement flame.
8:6

Many waters cannot quench love,
neither can the floods drown it:
if a man would give
all the wealth of his house for love,
it would utterly be rejected.
8:7

The Shulamite's Brothers:
We have a little sister,
and she has no breasts:
what shall we do for our sister in the day
when she shall be spoken for?
8:8

If she is a wall,
we will build upon her
towers of silver:
and if she is a door,
we will enclose her
with boards of cedar.
8:9

The Shulamite:
I am a wall,
and my breasts like towers:
then was I in his eyes
as one that found favor.
8:10

Solomon had a vineyard at Baalhamon;
he let out the vineyard unto keepers;
everyone for its fruit was
to bring a thousand pieces of silver.
8:11

(To Solomon):
My vineyard, which is mine, is before me:
you, O Solomon, must have a thousand,
and those that tend its fruit two hundred.
8:12

The Beloved:
You that dwell in the gardens,
the companions listen for your voice:
let me hear it.
8:13

The Shulamite:
Make haste, my beloved,
and be like a gazelle
or a young stag
upon the mountains of spices.
8:14

The love play continued, as the two discovered new horizons and explored new frontiers. It was a lifelong experience and a lifelong learning endeavor.

It was not their own love that they shared. It was the love that comes from God. There were no more two loves but one; no more two souls but one; no more two persons but one; no more two minds but one; no more two spirits but one; no more two goals but one.

Summary

The exposition of the storyline has been analyzed. The greatest love story on earth has finally been revealed. The dénouement has arrived.

The king and his wife demonstrate love in its most glorious form. Their love story transcends any love story we have ever heard. Their love journey takes us beyond the horizon, where no human has ever gone before. Their love shall be remembered and told for generations to come.

Their desire for each other stirred up and motivated their mutual attractions. Their love expressions transitioned from a gentle, dancelike, rhythmic tempo of excitement to a slow-paced love play as they entered the plateau phase. In ever-slower motions, their graceful maneuvers and plays gradually brought them to ever-higher levels of fantasies and excitements, punctuated by waves of her pleasures interspersed with his delights.

Under the apple tree, many skills and lessons have been learned. Yet, we are just beginning to understand how complex love can be.

Contrary to the contemporary ideal of achieving mutual satisfaction and fulfillment simultaneously, the couple took turns pleasing each other in their love expressions and bringing each other to ever-higher levels of enlightenment and blissful intimacy.

As one led, the other resonated. As one sacrificed, the other submitted. As one initiated, the other served. As one desired, the other fulfilled. Together, they journeyed into their oneness. They shared not two loves but one. They shared not two persons but one. In love, they trusted. In love they bonded. This love originates from God.

CHAPTER 8

Conclusion

Love the Lord your God with all your heart, and with all your soul, and with all your mind. . . . You shall love your neighbor as yourself.
Matthew 22:37, 39

Humanity is the highest of all God's creation, and God loves us more than anything else. Humans are the only beings God made to be like him—in his image and in his likeness. He gives humans authority over the plants and animals and over all his creation. However, we humans are poor managers. We pollute the air, the earth, and the oceans. We destroy human lives. We destroy the unborn. We make war instead of peace.

We are also poor managers of our own affairs and our own societies. With divorce rates skyrocketing, many marry with the worry that their marriages will not last. We Christians are at the crossroads. Instead of being light and salt to the world, we often find ourselves adopting the practices and norms of the world. Many of us even indulge in relationships and lifestyles that invite the wrath of our God.

We have sinned and fallen short of the glory (holiness) of God (Romans 3:23). Sin is the breaking of God's Ten Commandments, and it alienates us from God. The Bible tells us that the penalty for sin is death. But God foresaw our downfall and established a great plan for us. Jesus came into this world to sacrifice his own precious life for all who will believe in him and follow him. His sacrifice demonstrates his great love for humanity. It reestablishes our spiritual relationship with God when we believe in him. Jesus' sacrifice nurtures the bond between him as husband and the church as the bride.

Likewise, in marriage the husband demonstrates his love for his wife by making sacrifices for her. Working to earn for the family and helping in the family chores are not sacrifices; these are the results of Adam's downfall. Rather, Paul urges husbands to love their wives and genuinely sacrifice for them and serve them. Their attitude is to be that of Jesus himself, who said,

> "The Son of Man did not come to be served, but to serve, and to give His life a ransom for many." Matthew 20:28 (NKJV)

The woman was created as a "helper" and not as a mate or partner. She is to help her husband to achieve his desire, which is to please (serve) her. As a helper, she learns how to submit. It is through this submissiveness that the ultimate oneness can be achieved. Likewise, Christians learn how to submit to Jesus. His commands become our commands. And his commands are:

> *Love the Lord your God with all your heart, and with all your soul, and with all your mind. . . . You shall love your neighbor as yourself.*
> *Matthew 22:37, 39*

The more we love God, the more we want to please him, and follow Jesus, and be like him, and submit ourselves to him. Jesus says,

> *Go you into all the world, and preach the gospel to every creature.*
> *Mark 16:15*

This becomes our mission. From the submissiveness of the wife, we learn how to submit ourselves to Jesus and obey him. From the sacrificial, serving role of the husband, we understand more about how much Jesus loves us.

One crucial way the husband and wife's love is expressed is through the physical intimacy of sex. Indeed, without sex, the relationship between a man and a woman can be no more than that of friends. Only sex can bond the two persons in the oneness of husband and wife. Oneness amalgamates the husband and wife in terms of body, soul, and spirit such that they single-mindedly focus on achieving their common desire, with one leading while the other responds and helps.

The Song of Songs presents a beautiful biblical picture of physical intimacy in marriage. It reveals many secrets that are hidden to the casual reader. Sex is not about pleasure seeking or indulgence. It is about the sharing of love between husband and wife. If there were two loves, there would be differences. But there is only one love, and, as such, the differences disappear. Both husband and wife immerse themselves in this same melting pot of love. This is the love that originates from God and is designed by God. It is the love in which Jesus takes the leading role and the church the submissive role. It is the love that requires the husband to be the head and the wife to be the body. The leadership and the submissiveness reflect the mutual admiration and attraction between them that ultimately consolidates their mutual trust. Their mutual understanding and tender, loving care for each other transform the otherwise monotonous bedroom into one filled with music to the ears, the rhythms of pulsating heartbeats, and sparkles of admiration in their eyes. The leadership and submissiveness make possible the holistic union of two souls into one flesh.

The synergy of the duet in the lyrics of the Song of Songs echoes the vibrancy and coherence of their expressions. Contrary to the general perception that an ideal sexual outcome is simultaneous orgasm, the couple in the Song devote themselves wholeheartedly to taking turns in either giving or receiving in the love play. This allows them opportunities to learn and better understand each other's responses. We see in the Song that the wife's submissiveness is not passive. Quite often, a submissive wife takes the initiative in the expression of love. His responses to her initiatives and invitations reflect his voluntary support of the fulfillment of her desires, and her desire is toward encouraging him and helping him to fulfill his goals.

Sex is the means for husband and wife to enhance their delight in each other and build their love bonds. Sexual love is a lifelong learning process. The Song of Songs reveals many techniques employed by the couple. Obviously, they are not exhaustive, but they do set forth important examples to show us that sex is designed primarily for the expression of love. Reproduction is a by-product rather than the main course, which is in direct contradiction to general perception and Darwinian teaching.

By her submissiveness, the wife submerges herself into the oneness of love, progressing from "my beloved is mine, and I am his" to "I am my beloved's, and my beloved is mine" and ultimately to the holistic oneness of "I am my beloved's, and his desire is toward me." By the "apple tree" many more lessons and techniques are learned.

And so the Song continues. It marks only the beginning of the couple's love journey, which has no end. It also marks the beginning of their understanding of the love of their God. The apostle Paul summarizes most aptly:

This is a great mystery: but I speak concerning Christ and the church.
Ephesians 5:32

Let the love between husband and wife be the beginning of our understanding of the love of Jesus for his church. Indeed, this gives the purpose of earthly love a whole new dimension. We want to love God because he loved us first. We yearn to submit ourselves to Jesus.

Through circumcision Jewish males bore in their flesh a mark of God's promise, as well as a mark of their commitment to follow and love God. Christians, too, may choose circumcision as a symbol of their commitment to follow Jesus and be his spiritual leaders on earth.

Physical circumcision, however, is, and always has been, meaningless apart from circumcision of the heart. Circumcision of the heart is the love we have for God and for humanity. As we have seen, physical circumcision may help a husband to treat his wife with even greater tender, loving care. He can engage in sexual intercourse painlessly only when she is fully aroused. Thus, he learns to be patient. He learns how to sacrifice his own pleasure for her. As the head, he cherishes and nurtures her. In that sense, circumcision does have benefits. However, without circumcision of the heart, physical circumcision has no meaning and does more harm than good.

Circumcision does not provide salvation. The debate in Jerusalem (Acts 15:5–11) concluded that circumcision is optional. Thus, this should also render infant circumcision as optional. Circumcision is merely a reminder of one's promise and commitment to love God and serve him. Whether we have this physical sign in our bodies or not, as followers of Christ, we will want to keep his commandments, and we will want to keep our bodies holy.

Here, then, are the real secrets of fulfilling the divine purposes of that first love God established. We must *obey* him fully, recognizing that his commandments can be summed up in just two requirements: Love God, and love others as ourselves. In marriage, we must understand God's plan involves *sacrificial love* from the husband and *submissive love* from the wife. Adopting such roles manifests our obedience to God, our love for him and for one another, and our desire to grow toward *spiritual maturity* and its end result, *spiritual multiplication*. Finally, the love God intended to be expressed in marriage must include *physical intimacy* that is based on the selfless desire to please one's spouse.

The world views a husband and wife as two individuals, each with his or her own ambitions, self-interests, priorities, preferences, habits, and ideas. As followers of Christ, however, we see marriage as a three-tiered relationship (Jesus-husband-wife) that is not self-centered but selfless. We see Jesus as the head. He alone gives meaning and purpose to life. In him, husbands and wives pursue the same dreams and the goal of expanding the kingdom of God. Their personal ambitions and goals become of secondary importance, for they recognize the truth of Jesus' words:

> *"No man can serve two masters: for either he will hate the one, and love the other; or else he will hold to the one, and despise the other. You cannot serve God and mammon."*
> *Matthew 6:24*

INDEX

abraham
    circumcision and covenant *122-130*
    encountered with God *64-65*
    marriage made on earth *104-106*
    obedience *97-98*
    spiritual multiplication *113-124*
    ultimate test of faith *124*
adultery
    biblical definition *50*
    lust *167-168, 172*
    sex for avoidance *175*
    sins of the flesh *200*
    spiritual *82*
    ten commandment *33, 172*
aliens
    of the land *93-99*
    spiritual *106, 272*
all-inclusive
    love *83*
    worship and devotion *187*
allegorical interpretation *202, 209*
altar
    for sacrifice *124*
    for worship *127*
amalgamates the husband and wife *274*
anatomy
    knowledge for intimacy *47, 258*
    (See also: male reproductive system, female reproductive system)
anecdotal allegory of spiritual romance *211*
anti-circumcision *141*
apple
    euphemism *231, 252*
    tree *203, 224, 260-262, 269, 276*
arousal
    circumcision *216, 236*

in euphemism *222, 227, 232, 239, 240, 242*
in sexual response cycle *177-179, 181*
of clitoris *160*
of labia *161*
of penis *151-154*
of vagina *157*
techniques *190, 193, 219, 223-225*
assimilate *139*
ballooning *157, 178, 265*
baptism
    as symbol *49, 116, 134*
    not replacement for circumcision *135-136*
barzel *139*
baw-naw *(see: transform)*
bearer
    as commitments to God *142*
    of token of circumcision *127, 129*
bedroom
    confined within *87, 104, 109*
    outside *96*
birthright *127*
blood, in infant circumcision *142*
bloody husband *133-135*
body
    church *83, 115-117*
    earthly *69, 74*
    glorify God *90*
    in union of *164, 274*

holy *70*
of wife *76, 109*
power over *174-175*
submissive love *91, 100-102, 240-241*
boundary *15-16, 44*
bride
    flesh and bones *48*
    of Christ *81, 102-107*
    on first night *158, 218*
bridge *201*
brother
    as guardian *105, 219*
    husband as brother *257-258*
budded *249, 257*
caress
    alternating caressing *183*
    in foreplay *178*
    in prolonging plateau phase *181*
    in Song *224, 239, 243, 249, 253, 263*
celibacy *59, 80*
cervix *156*
Christ-like
    attributes *97, 95*
    of love *91, 166, 201*
circumcision
    as a bridge *146*
    controversies *27, 138*
    covenant *124-127, 135*
    effects of *154, 179, 189-193*
    female *143-144, 160*
    infant *141-143*

in Song *216, 236, 265-266*
of heart, as key secret to first love *128-130, 136, 166-168, 193-201*
of physical *131*
option *137-140, 145*
origin 132-134
spiritual *112, 135*
climax *152, (see also: ejaculation)*
clipped *132*
clitoris *159-160, 180-181, 264-265*
coagulation, of blood *144*
complementing, in submissiveness *100*
consummation *204, 232*
contour *264*
control
able women *21*
division of responsibilies 23
in plateau phase *179-181*
self *112*
to avoid temptations *170*
traits in a leader *82*
covenant
of circumcision *(see: circumcision)*
of marriage *49*
crawling *253*
dancing *251-253*
decircumcision *139*
dem-ooth *(see: likeness)*
demuth *(see: likeness)*

dilation, hymen *158, 243*
discharge
abnormal *184-185*
normal *156, 184*
divorce
as opposed to original intent *58*
extramarital *172*
no fault *9, 12*
not to *50*
rate *4, 5, 7, 27*
double-layered, of prepuce *151-152*
ecstasies *244*
ejaculate *(see: semen)*
ejaculation
common aim *183*
phase of sexual response cycle *181-182*
physiology of 150-151
sacrifice in Mosaic laws *183-189*
self-control *179, 180*
emission *181, 184, 186, 187, 188, 230*
emotions *53, 176, 181, 193-194, 207, 256*
endogamous marriage *10*
equality
in love relationship *44, 102, 174*
in society *21, 40, 43*
erection *153-154, 178, 189, 249, 250*
euphemism *135, 210, 214, 224, 233, 243*

281

fondle *178, 179, 180, 263*
foreskin *123, 132-134, 141, 151-154*
fornication *28, 50, 70, 75, 173, 175*
frenulum *139*
g-spot *157, 243*
galloping *264*
garden
    external *14*
    for special needs *39, 41, 45, 57, 60*
    in Song *239, 240, 243, 247, 249, 254, 257*
    means to show love *15, 42, 46*
    private *21*
gazelle *225, 227, 228, 237, 264*
genital
    emale *153, 180, 233, 239, 240, (see also: reproduction - system)*
    male *149, 235, 246, (see also: reproduction - system)*
glans *132, 139-141, 149, 151-154*
gospel
    bear fruits *116*
    free gift *117-119*
    Jesus' command *273*
    love Commandments *120-121*
    seed *113-114*

great mystery *57, 59-60, 73-80*
grip *157, 178, 180, 191*
gräfenberg *(see: g-spot)*
guardian *104-105, 219*
head-and-body relationship *86-88, 98, 100, 102*
headship
    leader *84-85, 102*
    of house *32*
    of wife *56*
    of Church *57, 76, 83-88*
    role *101, 172, 275*
    sacrifice *88-91,*
heart
    adultery *167*
    attitude of *165*
    believe *118*
    circumcision of *127-128, 131, 136, 145, 192-195*
    Holy Spirit filled *79*
    love God *30, 120, 198, 271, 276*
    lust *168*
    one another *166*
    purity *71*
    spiritual love *197*
    uncircumcised *199*
helper *47, 256, 273*
holiness
    body *70, 277*
    communion *33*
    keep day *31-32, 78*
    love *59, 73, 211*
    union (sex) *48, 58, 107, 175*

hoop-ak-oo *(see obey)*
hoop-ot-as *(see submissiveness)*
husband-and-wife relationship *43, 73, 112*
hymen *158, 243-244*
inspired *127, 205-206, 208, 210*
intercourse
   comfort *158*
   euphemism *244*
   in animals *164*
   Mosaic laws *184-189*
   pleasure *157*
   receptacle for *156*
   with circumcised *191*
   with uncircumcised *190*
jesus-husband-wife *278*
kissing *176,219*
labia
   majora *161, 237*
   minora *161, 191, 237, 264*
leadership
   circumcision *135*
   female *19*
   decision making *24*
   definition *84-85, 87-88*
   for binding *275*
   for mutual attraction *274*
   order of creation *41-42*
   one and only *43, 47*
   God given role *44, 56, 241*
   Jesus as example *102-104*

libido *177*
lifelong *164, 268, 275*
likeness *17-18, 60-63, 71-73*
lovemaking *176, 226*
lubrication *176-177, 216*
lust 69-77, *164-177, 197, 200*
master-and-slave *87, 117*
masturbation *132, 140, 187*
meatus *151, 246*
menstruation *155, 156*
missionary position *266*
multiplication *17, 34, 69, 111-112, 121-123, 130, 144*
mutilation *139*
narcotics anonymous *171*
nocturnal *(see emission)*
obedience
   by faith *135*
   Commandments *30, 120, 136*
   to God *14, 16, 28, 32, 34, 277*
   wife *29*
   to be seen *95-99*
oneness
   one-minded *256*
   head and body *86, 273*
   sexual union *102, 164, 176, 274*
   spiritual *201*
   submissiveness *275*
orgasm
   female *160, 190-191*
   in Song *227,234, 240, 246, 256, 259, 264, 275*

sexual response cycle *176, 179-189, 192*
tension *151*
ovaries *155*
palm tree *254-255*
penis *151-154*
polygamy *7*
priests and assistants *184, 187*
prostate gland *150*
pubic *160, 236, 247, 249, 251*
raisins *225, 231*
ransom *84-85, 273*
relaxation *(see resolution)*
repent *74, 119*
replenishing *33*
reproduction
    command *18*
    for oneness *164*
    for expression of love *275*
    for survival *22*
    system – female *155-161*
    system – male *149-154*
resolution *189, 228*
resonance *75, 143, 240, 256*
response
    by submission *76, 78*
    learning *104*
    physiological *176, 179, 202, 242*
    to God's love *47, 77*
    to the head *100, 143*
rhythm *249, 254, 269*
sacrifice
    of husband *85-86, 88-91, 109, 129, 179, 183-188, 256*
    of Jesus *55, 75*
scrotum *150, 249*
semen *153, 154, 159, 186, 178, 230-231*
seminal vesicles *150-151, 181*
sensation *128, 135, 149, 264*
sexaholics *172*
sexually transmitted disease *169*
shaft *132, 151-152, 154, 178, 190*
sins *118, 134, 137, 167-168, 184, 272*
sperm *150-151, 155, 182*
stimulation
    clitoris *158, 190*
    continuous *178*
    foreplay *177*
    for sustaining erection *250*
    G-spot *157-158*
    in prolonging love play *181*
    inner foreskin *154*
    labia minora *161*
    oral *216*
    taking turns *180*
    pause in *227*
stroking *178, 264*
subjection *(see: submission)*
submission *77, 76*

for conformation to local customs *94-100*
for love *91-93, 100-102*
subordinate *86, 100*
taboo *214, 220, 233, 259*
taste *80, 225*
techniques *234, 236, 258-260, 263-266, 275*
tension *151, 175, 264, 265*
tenting *157, 178, 265*
testicles *149, 150, 178, 181, 249-250*
thigh-to-thigh movement *178*
torso-to-torso rubbing *178*
tugging and pulling of the lips *159*
uncircumcision *127, 136-137, 140, 154, 190*

urinary bladder *150*
uterus *155-156*
vagina
    anatomy *155-159*
    excitement state *180*
    intercourse *182, 190-191*
    lubrication *178*
    stretching *243*
virginity *219, 239, 244*
vulva *155, 239, 240, 244, 253*
womb (see: uterus)
worship
    church *33*
    cleanness *182, 185*
    God *29, 62, 127, 194*
    Holy of holies *193*
    in spirit *63*

REFERENCE

[1] See, for example, Susan Waggoner, *I Do! I Do! The Origins of 100 Classic Wedding Traditions* (New York: Rizzoli Publications, 2002); and Tiziana Baldizzone and Gianni Baldizzone, *Wedding Ceremonies: Ethnic Symbols, Costume and Rituals* (Paris: Flammarion, 2001).

[2] Institute for American Values and the National Center on African American Marriages and Parenting, "The Marriage Index: A Proposal to Establish Leading Marriage Indicators," *American Values Investments: www.americanvalues.com*.

[3] Roberta L. Coles and Charles Green, eds., *The Myth of the Missing Black Father* (New York: Columbia University Press, 2010), 125-26; *Current Population Survey, 2006 Annual Social and Economic (ASEC) Supplement* (PDF) (Washington, DC: United States Bureau of the Census, 2006), cited in "Single Parent," *Wikipedia.com: www.wikipedia.com*.

[4] P. Butterworth, "Multiple and severe disadvantage in receiving income support," *Family Matters* 64:22-29.

[5] "One-Parent Families," *Canberra Times*, 23 July 2008, http://www.abs.gov.au/AUSSTATS/abs@.nsf/Latestproducts/F4B15 (April 6, 2009).

[6] Australian Council of Social Service, "Facts about Single Parent

Families and Welfare," Strawberry Hills, NSW, 2005, http://search.informit.com.au/documentSummary;dn=213328295148297;res=IELHSS.

[7] David de Vaus, *Diversity and Change in Australian Families: Statistical Profiles* (Melbourne: Australian Institute of Family Studies, 2004), 51-53. Australian Government: http://www.aifs.gov.au/institute/pubs/diversity/main.html (November 15, 2013).

[8] K. D. Crowder and S. E. Tolnay, "A New Marriage Squeeze for Black Women: The Role of Racial Intermarriage by Black men," *Journal of Marriage and Family* 62:792-807.

[9] *Relationships Indicators Survey 1998* (Relationships Australia, 1998), 2.

[10] W. B. Wilcox, "The Evolution of Divorce," *National Affairs,* Issue 1, Fall 2009. National Affairs: http://www.nationalaffairs.com/publications/detail/the-evolution-of-divorce (August 20, 2011).

[11] Barbara Hargrave, "Gender, the Family and the Sacred," in *The Sacred in a Secular Age,* ed. P. E. Hammond (Berkeley: University of California Press, 1985), 206.

[12] T. B. Heaton, "Religious Group Characteristics, Endogamy, and Interfaith Marriage," *Sociological Analysis* 51(4): 363-76.

[13] Andrew Cherlin, *Public and Private Families: An Introduction,* 4th ed. (New York: McGraw-Hill, 2004), 234; Bahira Sherif Trask and Tara Woolfolk, "Trends in Marriage and Cohabitation," in *Cultural Diversity and Families: Expanding Perspectives,* ed. Bahira Sherif Trask and Raeann R. Hamon (Thousand Oaks, CA: Sage Publications, 2007), 80.

[14] W. L. Rogers and A. Thornton, "Changing Patterns of First Marriage in the United States," *Demography* 22(2): 265-79; Joshua R. Goldstein and Catherine T. Kenney, "Marriage Delayed or Marriage Forgone? New Cohort Forecasts of First Marriage for U.S. Women," *American Sociological Review* 66(4):

506-19.

[15] ChristianAnswers.net, "Women of the Bible," WebBible Encyclopedia, *Christian Answers:* http://www.christiananswers.net/dictionary/women.html (September 20, 2010).

[16] United States Department of Commerce, *Statistical Abstract of the United States: 2009: The National Data Book* (Baton Rouge: Claitors, 2008), 183.

[17] K. A. Mathews, *Genesis 1-11:26*, The New American Commentary. Nashville: Broadman and Holman, 1996), 26-41.

[18] Adam Clarke, *The Adam Clarke Commentary*, on Ephesians 5:16, StudyLight.org: http://www.studylight.org/com/acc/view.cgi?bk=48&ch=5

[19] John Gill, *John Gill's Exposition of the Entire Bible* (e-Sword version).

[20] Raymond C. Ortlund Jr., *God's Unfaithful Wife: A Biblical Theology of Spiritual Adultery* (Downers Grove, IL: IVP Academic, 2003), 47-76.

[21] Martin Chemers, *An Integrative Theory of Leadership* (Mahwah, NJ: Lawrence Erlbaum Associates, 1997), 20; R. M. Stogdill, "Personal Factors Associated with Leadership: A Survey of the Literature," *Journal of Psychology* 25:35-71.

[22] Shaye J. D. Cohen, *Why Aren't Jewish Women Circumcised? Gender and Covenant in Judaism* (Berkeley: University of California Press, 2005), 95.

[23] An Egyptian hieroglyph and tomb artwork from the Sixth Dynasty (2345-2181 BCE) show circumcised men; see James H. Breasted, *The Dawn of Conscience,* (New York: Scribner's, 1933), 10.

[24] Paul Johnson, *A History of the Jews* (London: Phoenix Press, 1993), 37.

[25] J. Richters, et al., "Circumcision in Australia: Prevalence and Effects on Sexual Health," *International Journal of STD AIDS*

17(8): 547–554.

[26] W. D. Dunsmuir and E. M. Gordon, "The History of Circumcision." *BJU International* 83.1 (1999): 1–12.

[27] TH Hull and M. Budiharsana, "Male Circumcision and Penis Enhancement in Southeast Asia: Matters of Pain and Pleasure." *Reproductive Health Matters* 9(18): 60–67.

[28] A. Thomas, *Circumcision: An Ethnomedical Study* (Longdon: The Gilgal Society, 2003).

[29] Herodotus, *The Histories,* trans. by A. D. Godley (Cambridge, MA: Harvard University Press, 1920), 1:199.

[30] Theodore James, "Philo on Circumcision" *South African Mediese Tydskrif,* August 21, 1976: 1411.

[31] Brian J. Morris, Alex D. Wodak, et al., "Infant Male Circumcision: An Evidence-based Policy Statement," *Open Journal of Preventive Medicine* 2:1 (2012): 79–92.

[32] Karen Ericksen Paige, "The Ritual of Circumcision," *Human Nature,* May 1978, pp. 40–48.

[33] Felix Bryk, *Circumcision in Man and Woman: Its History, Psychology and Ethnology* (New York: American Ethnological Press, 1934), 102–3.

[34] E. A. Wallis Budge, The Gods of the Egyptians, vol 1. (New York: Dover, 1969), 30–31.

[35] David L. Gollaher, *Circumcision: A History of the World's Most Controversial Surgery* (New York: Basic Books, 2000), 30–33.

[36] See statuette of Merire-hashetef, from the Egyptian Museum, Cairo, in David A. Bolnick, Martin A. Koyle, and Assaf Yosha, eds., *Surgical Guide to Circumcision* (London: Springer-Verlag, 2012), ebook edition, 246.

[37] James E. Peron, "Circumcision: Then and Now," *Many Blessings* (Spring 2000) III:41–42.

[38] Leonard B. Glick, *Marked in Your Flesh: Circumcision from Ancient Judea to Modern America* (New York: Oxford University

Press, 2006), 44.

[39] See "Circumcision," *Jewish Virtual Library:* *http://www.jewishvirtuallibrary.org/jsource/judaica/ejud_0002_000 4_0_04318.html* (December 6, 2013); "Methods of Circumcision," *Circumstitions.com:* *http://www.circumstitions.com/methods.html#barzel* (December 6, 2013); "Circumcision," *Jewish Encyclopedia:* *http://www.jewishencyclopedia.com/articles/4391-circumcision* (December 6, 2013).

[40] S. I. McMillen, *None of these Diseases* (Old Tappan, NJ: Revell, 1963).

[41] Peter Remondino, *History of Circumcision, from the Earliest Times to the Present* (Philadelphia: F.A. Davis, 1891).

[42] Peron, "Circumcision: then and now."

[43] J. N. Krieger, "Male Circumcision and HIV Infection Risk," *World Journal of Urology* 30(1): 3–13; J. Hutchinson, "On the Influence of Circumcision in Preventing Syphilis," *Medical Times Gazette* NS Vol II: 542–43; N. Siegfried, M. Muller, J. J. Deeks, and J. Volmick, "Male Circumcision for Prevention of Heterosexual Acquisition of HIV in Men," *Cochrane Database of Systematic Reviews* April 15, 2009 (2): CD003362.

[44] Carina Storrs, "Clean-Cut: Study Finds Circumcision Helps Prevent HIV," *Scientific America* (January 13, 2010), 27; Barbara Juncosa, "Fact or Fiction: Does Circumcision Help Prevent HIV Infection?" *Scientific America* (December 1, 2008), 31.

[45] M. S. Brown and C. A. Brown, "Circumcision Decision: Prominence of Social Concerns," *Pediatrics* 80(2): 215–219.

[46] J. D. Tiemstra, "Factors Affecting the Circumcision Decision," *Journal of the American Board of Family Practice* 12(1): 16–20.

[47] World Health Organization and UNAIDS. *Neonatal and Child Male Circumcision: A Global Review* (Joint United Nations Programme on HIV/AIDS (UNAIDS), 2010).

[48] Isabella Shepherd, "A Study of the Effect of Vitamin K upon

Neonatal Survival in African and Indian Patients, *South African Medical Journal* 7 (November 1959): 946.

[49] WordNet Search, "Birth Canal," *WordNetSearch*: http://wordnetweb.princeton.edu/perl/webwn?s=birth%20canal (June 13, 2012).

[50] A. Salonia, A. Giraldi, et al., "Physiology of Women's Sexual Function: Basic Knowledge and New Findings," *Journal of Sex Medicine* 7:2637–2660; Susan A. Orshan, *Maternal, Newborn, And Women's Health Nursing: Comprehensive Care Across The Lifespan* (Philadelphia: Lippincott Williams and Wilkins, 2006).

[51] Clifford Penner and Joyce Penner, *The Gift of Sex: A Guide to Sexual Fulfilment* (Nashville: Thomas Nelson, 2003).

[52] Michai Kilchevsky, Yoram Vardi, Lior Lowenstein, and Ilan Gruenwald, "Is the Female G-Spot Truly a Distinct Anatomic Entity?" *The Journal of Sexual Medicine* 9(3): 719–726.

[53] T. Hines, "The G-Spot: A Modern Gynecologic Myth," *American Journal of Obstetrics Gynecology* 185(2): 359–62.

[54] M. Douglas Moore, *First Night and Beyond: A Guide to Intimacy and Sexual Fulfillment for Newlyweds* (Provo, UT: Moore Heart Enterprises, 2002); Scott Farhart and Elizabeth King, *The Christian Woman's Complete Guide to Health: Everything You Need to Know About You! Adolescence to Menopause and Everything in Between* (Lake Mary, FL: Siloam Press, 2008); Ed Wheat and Gaye Wheat, *Intended for Pleasure: Sex Technique and Sexual Fulfillment in Christian Marriage* (Grand Rapids: Revell, 1997).

[55] H. E. O'Connell, K. V. Sanjeevan, et al., "Anatomy of the Clitoris," *Journal of Urology* 174(4): 1189–95.

[56] Merriam Webster, "Lust," *Merriam Webster*: http://www.merriam-webster.com/dictionary/lust (October 8, 2012).

[57] P. D. Borman and D. N. Dixon, "Spirituality and the 12 Steps of Substance Abuse Recovery," *Journal of Psychology & Theology* 26(3): 287–91; "Twelve Steps and Twelve Traditions,"

Alcoholics Anonymous World Services, Inc., 1989.

[58] Ernest Kurtz, "Alcoholics Anonymous and the Disease Concept of Alcoholism," *Alcoholism Treatment Quarterly* 20 (3–4): 5–39.

[59] Wikipedia, "Twelve-step program," *Wikipedia.com*: http://en.wikipedia.org/wiki/Twelve-step_program (October 30, 2012).

[60] Hal Arkowitz and Scott O. Lilienfeld, "Does Alcoholics Anonymous Work?" *Scientific America* March 29, 2011; Kim Dennis, "Food and Addiction Spectrum Disorders," 2012 Annual Midwest Eating Disorders Conference, Marriott Oakbrook.

[61] Jeffrey M. Brandsma and M. Dicarli, "Toward a More Rational Alcoholics Anonymous," *Rational Living* 11(1): 35–37; S. Imber, E. Schultz, F. Funderburk, R. Allen, and R. Flamer, "The Fate of the Untreated Alcoholic," *Journal of Nervous and Mental Disorders* 162:238–47; B. Kissin, A. Platz, and W. H. Su, "Social and Psychological Factors in the Treatment of Chronic Alcoholics," *Journal of Psychiatric Research* 8:13–27.

[62] C. K. Williams, "Pre-Roman Cults in the Area of the Forum of Ancient Corinth," (Ph.D. Dissertation, University of Pennsylvania, 1978), 49.

[63] *Herodotus: The Histories,* translated by A. D. Godley, Loeb Classical Library (Cambridge, MA: Harvard University Press, 1920), 1.199; see also Wikipedia, "Sacred prostitution," *Wikipedia.com*: http://en.wikipedia.org/wiki/Sacred_prostitution#cite_note-6. (November 20, 2012).

[64] William H. Masters and Virginia E. Johnson, *Human Sexual Response* (New York: Bantam, 1981); see Wikipedia, "Human sexual response cycle," *Wikipedia.com*: http://en.wikipedia.org/wiki/Human_sexual_response_cycle#cite_note-Archer.2C_Lloyd-1 (March 3, 2013): "The human sexual response cycle is a four-stage model of physiological

responses during sexual stimulation. These phases, in order of their occurrence, are the excitement phase, plateau phase, orgasmic phase, and resolution phase."

[65] Helen Singer Kaplan, *Disorders of Sexual Desire* (New York: Brunner/Mazel, 1979). See also Jerrold S. Greenberg, Clint E. Bruess, and Sarah C. Conklin, *Exploring the Dimensions of Human Sexuality*, 4th ed. (London: Jones and Burtlett Publishers, London, 2010), 160-61.

[66] Brandon Keim, "Female Orgasm Remains an Evolutionary Mystery," *Wired Science*, 6 September 2011.

[67] Brendan P. Zietsch, Geoffrey F. Miller, et al., "Female Orgasm Rates are Largely Independent of Other Traits: Implications for 'Female Orgasmic Disorder' and Evolutionary Theories of Orgasm," *The Journal of Sexual Medicine* 8(8): 2305–16.

[68] R. J. Kevin, "Can the Controversy about the Putative Role of the Human Female Orgasm in Sperm Transport Be Settled with Our Current Physiological Knowledge of Coitus?" *The Journal of Sexual Medicine* 8(6): 1566–78.

[69] Elisabeth A. Lloyd, *The Case of the Female Orgasm: Bias in the Science of Evolution* (Harvard University Press, 2005).

[70] Gary W. Demarest, *Leviticus, The Preacher's Commentary* (Nashville: Nelson, 2002; e-Sword version).

[71] C. F. Keil and Franz Delitzsch, *Keil and Delitzsch Commentary on the Old Testament* (e-sword version): "Involuntary emission of seed"; Gill, *John Gill's Exposition of the Entire Bible* (e-Sword version): "And if any man's seed of copulation go out from him . . . Not in lawful cohabitation, nor voluntarily, but involuntarily . . . not through any disorder . . . but through a dream, or any lustful imagination; what is commonly called nocturnal pollution."

[72] John C. Maxwell, *Deuteronomy, The Preachers Commentary* (Nashville: Nelson, 2002; e-sword version); Michael Morrison, *Sabbath, Circumcision, and Tithing: Which Old Testament Laws*

Apply to Christians? (Linoln, NE: iUniverse, 2002), 203.

[73] Lloyd, "The Case of the Female Orgasm."

[74] J. A. Flaherty J. M. Davis, et al., *Psychiatry: Diagnosis & Therapy* (East Norwalk, CT: Appleton & Lange, 1993), 217.

[75] M. Friedlander, *The Jewish Religion* (London: Shapiro, Vallentine & Co., 1922), cited in Irene Lipson, *The Greatest Commandment* (Clarksville, MD: Lederer Books, Messianic Jewish Publishers, 2007), 6.

[76] Lipson, *The Greatest Commandment*, 57–63.

[77] Albert Barnes, *Albert Barnes' Notes on the Bible* (e-sword version).

[78] Among those who take this approach are Joseph C. Dillow, *Solomon on Sex* (Nashville: Thomas Nelson, 1982); and Douglas E. Rosenau, *A Celebration of Sex: A Guide to Enjoying God's Gift of Sexual Intimacy* (Nashville: Thomas Nelson, 2002).

[79] New King James Version, footnote at Song of Songs,.

[80] This procedure is described in chapter 5.

[81] David A. Hubbard, *Ecclesiastes/Song of Solomon, The Preacher's Commentary* (Nashville: Nelson, 2002; e-sword version).

CPSIA information can be obtained
at www.ICGtesting.com
Printed in the USA
LVOW12s1435090517
533870LV00001B/117/P